The Wild-Goose Chase by John Fletcher

John Fletcher was born in December, 1579 in Rye, Sussex. He was baptised on December 20th.

As can be imagined details of much of his life and career have not survived and, accordingly, only a very brief indication of his life and works can be given.

Young Fletcher appears at the very young age of eleven to have entered Corpus Christi College at Cambridge University in 1591. There are no records that he ever took a degree but there is some small evidence that he was being prepared for a career in the church.

However what is clear is that this was soon abandoned as he joined the stream of people who would leave University and decamp to the more bohemian life of commercial theatre in London.

The upbringing of the now teenage Fletcher and his seven siblings now passed to his paternal uncle, the poet and minor official Giles Fletcher. Giles, who had the patronage of the Earl of Essex may have been a liability rather than an advantage to the young Fletcher. With Essex involved in the failed rebellion against Elizabeth Giles was also tainted.

By 1606 John Fletcher appears to have equipped himself with the talents to become a playwright. Initially this appears to have been for the Children of the Queen's Revels, then performing at the Blackfriars Theatre.

Fletcher's early career was marked by one significant failure; The Faithful Shepherdess, his adaptation of Giovanni Battista Guarini's Il Pastor Fido, which was performed by the Blackfriars Children in 1608.

By 1609, however, he had found his stride. With his collaborator John Beaumont, he wrote Philaster, which became a hit for the King's Men and began a profitable association between Fletcher and that company. Philaster appears also to have begun a trend for tragicomedy.

By the middle of the 1610s, Fletcher's plays had achieved a popularity that rivalled Shakespeare's and cemented the pre-eminence of the King's Men in Jacobean London. After his frequent early collaborator John Beaumont's early death in 1616, Fletcher continued working, both singly and in collaboration, until his own death in 1625. By that time, he had produced, or had been credited with, close to fifty plays.

Index of Contents

DRAMATIS PERSONAE

De-Gard, A Noble stay'd' Gentleman that being newly lighted from his Travels, assists his Sister Oriana in her chase of Mirabel the Wild-Goose.

La-Castre, the Indulgent Father to Mirabell.

Mirabell, the Wild-Goose, a Travell'd Monsieur, and great defyer of all Ladies in the way of Marriage, otherwise their much loose servant, at last caught by the despis'd Oriana.

Pinac, his fellow Traveller, of a lively spirit, and Servant to the no less sprightly Lillia-Bianca.

Belleur, Companion to both, of a stout blunt humour, in love with Rosalura.

Nantolet, Father to Rosalura and Lillia-Bianca.

Lugier, the rough and confident Tutor to the Ladies, and chief Engine to entrap the Wild-Goose.

Oriana, the fair betroth'd of Mirabell, and witty follower of the Chase.

Rosalura   } the Airie Daughters of Nantolet.
Lillia-Bianca   }

Petella, their Waiting-woman.

Mariana, an English Courtezan.

A young Factor.

Page.

Servants.

Singing-Boy.

Two Merchants.

Priest.

Four Women.

THE SCENE: Paris.

Enter **MONSIEUR De GARD**, and a Foot-**BOY**.

De GARD
Sirrah, you know I have rid hard; stir my Horse well
And let him want no Litter.

BOY
I am sure I have run hard,
Would some body would walk me, & see me Litter'd;
For I think my fellow-horse, cannot in reason
Desire more rest, nor take up his Chamber before me,
But we are the Beasts now, and the Beasts are our Masters.

De GARD
When you have done, step to the Ten-Crown Ordinary.

BOY
With all my heart, Sir,
For I have a Twenty Crown stomach.

De GARD
And there bespeak a dinner.

BOY
Yes Sir, presently.

De GARD
For whom, I beseech you, Sir?

BOY
For my self, I take it, Sir.

De GARD
In truth ye shall not take it, 'tis not meant for you,
There's for your Provender: Bespeak a Dinner
For Monsieur Mirabell, and his Companions,
They'll be in Town within this hour.
When you have done, Sirrah,
Make ready all things at my Lodging, for me,
And wait me there.

BOY
The Ten Crown Ordinary?

De GARD
Yes Sir, if you have not forgot it.

BOY
I'le forget my feet first;
'Tis the best part of a Foot-mans faith.

[Exit **BOY**.

De GARD
These youths
For all they have been in Italy, to learn thrift,
And seem to wonder at mens lavish waies,
Yet they cannot rub off old friends, their French itches;
They must meet sometimes to disport their Bodies
With good Wine, and good Women; and good store too.
Let 'em be what they will, they are Arm'd at all points,
And then hang saving. Let the Sea grow high,
This Ordinary can fit 'em of all sizes,

[Enter **La-CASTRE** and **ORIANA**.

They must salute their Country with old customes.

ORIANA
Brother.

De GARD
My dearest Sister.

ORIANA
Welcome, welcome:
Indeed ye are welcome home, most welcome.

De GARD
Thank ye,
You are grown a handsome woman, Oriana,
(Blush at your faults) I am wondrous glad to see ye.
Monsieur La-Castre: Let not my Affection
To my fair Sister, make me be held unmannerly:
I am glad to see ye well, to see ye lusty,
Good health about ye, and in fair company,
Believe me, I am proud—

La-CASTRE
Fair Sir, I thank ye:
Monsieur de Gard, you are welcome from your journey,
Good men, have still good welcome: give me your hand, Sir.

Once more, you are welcome home: you look still younger.

De GARD
Time has no leasure to look after us.
We wander every where: Age cannot find us.

La-CASTRE
And how does all?

De GARD
All well, Sir; and all lusty.

La-CASTRE
I hope my Son be so, I doubt not, Sir,
But you have often seen him in your journeys,
And bring me some fair News.

De GARD
Your Son is well, Sir,
And grown a proper Gentleman: he is well, and lusty,
Within this eight hours, I took leave of him,
And over-ey'd him, having some slight business
That forc'd me out o'th' way: I can assure you
He will be here to night.

La-CASTRE
Ye make me glad, Sir,
For o' my faith, I almost long to see him,
Me thinks he has been away—

De GARD
'Tis but your tenderness;
What are three years? a love-sick wench will allow it:
His friends that went out with him are come back too;
Belleur, and young Pinac: he bid me say little,
Because he means to be his own glad Messenger.

La-CASTRE
I thank ye for this news, Sir, he shall be welcome,
And his friends too: indeed I thank you heartily:
And how (for I dare say, you will not flatter him)
Has Italy wrought on him? has he mew'd yet
His wild fantastick Toyes? they say that Climate
Is a great purger of those humorous Fluxes.
How is he improved, I pray ye?

De GARD
No doubt, Sir, well.

H'as born himself a full, and noble Gentleman,
To speak him farther is beyond my Charter.

La-CASTRE
I am glad to hear so much good; Come, I see
You long to enjoy your Sister: yet I must intreat ye
Before I go, to sup with me to night
And must not be deni'd.

De GARD
I am your servant.

La-CASTRE
Where you shall meet fair, merry, and noble Company.
My neighbour Natolet, and his two fair Daughters.

De GARD
Your supper's season'd well, Sir. I shall wait upon ye.

La-CASTRE
Till then I'le leave ye: and y'are once more welcome.

De GARD
I thank ye, noble Sir. Now, Oriana,

[Exit.

How have ye done since I went? have ye had your health well?
And your mind free?

ORIANA
You see I am not bated;
Merry, and eat my meat.

De GARD
A good preservative.
And how have you been us'd? You know, Oriana,
Upon my going out, at your request,
I left your Portion in La-Castre's hands,
(The main Means you must stick to) for that reason
(And 'tis no little one) I ask ye, Sister,
With what humanity he entertains ye,
And how ye find his courtesie?

ORIANA
Most ready.
I can assure you, Sir, I am us'd most nobly.

De GARD

I am glad to hear it: But I prethee tell me,
(And tell me true) what end had you, Oriana,
In trusting your mony here? He is no Kinsman,
Nor any tie upon him of a Guardian;
Nor dare I think ye doubt my prodigality.

ORIANA

No, certain, Sir, none of all this provoked me;
Another private reason.

De GARD

'Tis not private,
Nor carryed so: 'tis common (my fair Sister)
Your love to Mirabel; your blushes tell it:
'Tis too much known, and spoken of too largely;
And with no little shame I wonder at it.

ORIANA

Is it a shame to love?

De GARD

To love undiscreetly:
A Virgin should be tender of her honour,
Close, and secure.

ORIANA

I am as close as can be,
And stand upon as strong and honest guards too;
Unless this Warlike Age need a Port-cullis:
Yet I confess, I love him.

De GARD

Hear the people.

ORIANA

Now I say hang the people: He that dares
Believe what they say, dares be mad, and give
His Mother, nay his own Wife up to Rumor;
All grounds of truth they build on, is a Tavern,
And their best censure's Sack, Sack in abundance:
For as they drink, they think: they ne're speak modestly
Unless the wine be poor, or they want mony.
Believe them? believe Amadis de Gaul,
The Knight o'th' Sun, or Palmerin of England;
For these, to them, are modest, and true stories.
Pray understand me; if their tongues be truth,
And if in Vino veritas be an Oracle,

What Woman is, or has been ever honest?
Give 'em but ten round cups, they'll swear Lucretia
Dy'd not for want of power to resist Tarquin,
But want of Pleasure, that he stay'd no longer:
And Portia, that was famous for her Piety
To her lov'd Lord, they'll face ye out, dy'd o'th' Pox.

De GARD
Well, there is something, Sister.

ORIANA
If there be, Brother,
'Tis none of their things, 'tis not yet so monstrous;
My thing is Marriage: And at his return
I hope to put their squint-eyes right again.

De GARD
Marriage? 'tis true; his Father is a rich man;
Rich both in land and money: he his heir,
A young and handsome man, I must confess too;
But of such qualities, and such wild flings,
Such admirable imperfections, Sister,
(For all his Travel, and bought experience)
I should be loth to own him for my Brother:
Methinks a rich mind in a state indifferent
Would prove the better fortune.

ORIANA
If he be wild,
The reclaiming him to good, and honest, (Brother)
Will make much for my honour; which, if I prosper,
Shall be the study of my love, and life too.

De GARD
Ye say well; would he thought as well, and loved too.
He Marry? he'll be hanged first: he knows no more
What the conditions and the ties of Love are,
The honest purposes and grounds of Marriage,
Nor will know, nor be ever brought t' endeavour,
Than I do how to build a Church; he was ever
A loose and strong defier of all order,
His Loves are wanderers, they knock at each door,
And taste each dish, but are no residents:
Or say he may be brought to think of Marriage,
(As 'twill be no small labour) thy hopes are strangers.
I know there is a labour'd match, now follow'd,
(Now at this time, for which he was sent for home too)
Be not abus'd, Natolet has two fair Daughters,

And he must take his choice.

ORIANA
Let him take freely;
For all this I despair not; my mind tells me
That I, and only I, must make him perfect;
And in that hope I rest.

De GARD
Since y'are so confident,
Prosper your hope; I'll be no adversary;
Keep your self fair and right, he shall not wrong ye.

ORIANA
When I forget my vertue, no man know me.

[Exeunt.

SCÆNA SECUNDA

Enter **MIRABELL**, **PINAC**, **BELLEUR** and **SERVANTS**.

MIRABELL
Welcome to Paris once more, Gentlemen;
We have had a merry and a lusty Ordinary,
And Wine, and good meat, and a bounsing Reckoning;
And let it go for once; 'Tis a good Physick,
Only the Wenches are not for my diet,
They are too lean and thin; their embraces brawn-faln.
Give me the plump Venetian, fat, and lusty,
That meets me soft and supple; smiles upon me,
As if a Cup of full Wine leapt to kiss me;
These slight things I affect not.

PINAC
They are ill built;
Pin-buttockt, like your dainty Barbaries,
And weak i'th' pasterns; they'll endure no hardness.

MIRABELL
There's nothing good, or handsom bred amongst us:
Till we are travel'd, and live abroad, we are Coxcombs:
Ye talk of France, a slight unseason'd Country,
Abundance of gross food, which makes us Block-heads:
We are fair set out indeed, and so are fore-horses:
Men say we are great Courtiers, men abuse us:

We are wise, and valiant too, non credo, Seignior:
Our Women the best Linguists, they are Parrats;
O' this side the Alpes they are nothing but meer Drolleries:
Ha, Roma la Santa, Italy for my money,
Their policies, their customs, their frugalities,
Their courtesies so open, yet so reserved too,
As when ye think y'are known best, ye are a stranger;
The very pick-teeth speak more man than we do,
And season of more salt.

PINAC
'Tis a brave Country:
Not pester'd with your stubborn precise Puppies,
That turn all useful and allow'd contentments
To scabs and scruples; hang 'em Capon-worshippers.

BELLEUR
I like that freedom well, and like their Women too,
And would fain do as others do; but I am so bashful,
So naturally an Ass: Look ye, I can look upon 'em,
And very willingly I go to see 'em,
(There's no man willinger) and I can kiss 'em,
And make a shift—

MIRABELL
But if they chance to flout ye,
Or say ye are too bold; fie, Sir, remember;
I pray sit farther off;—

BELLEUR
'Tis true, I am humbled,
I am gone, I confess ingenuously I am silenced,
The spirit of Amber cannot force me answer.

PINAC
Then would I sing and dance.

BELLEUR
You have wherewithal, Sir.

PINAC
And charge her up again.

BELLEUR
I can be hang'd first;
Yet where I fasten well I am a tyrant.

MIRABELL

Why, thou darst fight?

BELLEUR
Yes, certainly, I dare fight;
And fight with any man at any weapon,
Would the other were no more; but a pox on't,
When I was sometimes in my height of hope,
And reasonable valiant that way, my heart harden'd,
Some scornful jest or other chops between me
And my desire: what would ye have me to do then, Gentlemen?

MIRABELL
Belvere, you must be bolder: Travel three years,
And bring home such a Baby to betray ye
As bashfulness? a great fellow, and a Souldier?

BELLEUR
You have the gift of impudence, be thankful;
Every man has not the like talent: I will study
And if it may be reveal'd to me.

MIRABELL
Learn of me,
And of Pinac: no doubt you'll find employment;
Ladies will look for Courtship.

PINAC
'Tis but fleshing,
But standing one good brunt or two: hast thou any mind to marriage?
We'l provide thee some soft-natur'd wench, that's dumb too.

MIRABELL
Or an old woman that cannot refuse thee in charity.

BELLEUR
A dumb woman, or an old woman, that were eager
And car'd not for Discourse, I were excellent at.

MIRABELL
You must now put on boldness, there's no avoiding it;
And stand all hazards; flye at all games bravely;
They'll say you went out like an Oxe, and return'd like an Ass else.

BELLEUR
I shall make danger sure.

MIRABELL
I am sent for home now,

I know it is to marry, but my Father shall pardon me,
Although it be a witty Ceremony,
And may concern me hereafter in my Gravity;
I will not lose the freedom of a Traveller;
A new strong lusty Bark cannot ride at one Anchor;
Shall I make divers suits to shew to the same eyes?
'Tis dull and home-spun; Study several pleasures,
And want employments for 'em? I'll be hang'd first;
Tye me to one smock? make my travels fruitless?
I'll none of that; for every fresh behaviour,
By your leave, Father, I must have a fresh Mistriss,
And a fresh favour too.

BELLEUR
I like that passingly;
As many as you will, so they be willing,
Willing, and gentle, gentle.

PINAC
There's no reason
A Gentleman, and a Traveller should be clapt up,
For 'tis a kind of Bæboes to be married
Before he manifest to the World his good parts:
Tug ever like a Rascal at one Oar?
Give me the Italian liberty.

MIRABELL
That I study;
And that I will enjoy; Come, go in Gentlemen,
There mark how I behave my self, and follow.

[Exeunt.

SCÆNIA TERTIA

Enter **LA-CASTRE, NATOLET, LUGIER, ROSALURA, LILLIA-BIANCA.**

La-CASTRE
You and your beauteous daughters are most welcome,
Beshrew my blood they are fair ones; welcom Beauties,
Welcome, sweet Birds.

NATOLET
They are bound much to your courtesies.

La-CASTRE

I hope we shall be nearer acquainted.

NATOLET

That's my hope too.
For certain, Sir, I much desire your Alliance:
You see 'em, they are no Gypsies, for their breeding,
It has not been so coarse, but they are able
To rank themselves with women of fair fashion;
Indeed they have been trained well.

LUGIER

Thank me.

NATOLET

Fit for the Heirs of that State I shall leave 'em;
To say more, is to sell 'em. They say your Son
Now he has travell'd must be wondrous curious,
And choice in what he takes: these are no coarse ones;
Sir, here's a merry wench, let him look to himself,
(All heart, i'faith) may chance to startle him;
For all his care, and travell'd caution,
May creep into his Eye; if he love Gravity,
Affect a solemn face, there's one will fit him.

La-CASTRE

So young, and so demure?

NATOLET

She is my Daughter,
Else I would tell you, Sir, she is a Mistriss
Both of those manners and that modesty
You would wonder at: She is no often Speaker,
But when she does, she speaks well; Nor no Reveller,
Yet she can dance, and has studied the Court Elements,
And sings, as some say, handsomely; if a woman,
With the decency of her Sex, may be a Scholar,
I can assure ye, Sir, she understands too.

La-CASTRE

These are fit Garments, Sir.

LUGIER

Thank them that cut 'em;
Yes, they are handsome women; they have handsome parts too;
Pretty becoming parts.

La-CASTRE

'Tis like they have, Sir.

LUGIER
Yes, yes, and handsome Education they have had too,
Had it abundantly; they need not blush at it;
I taught it, I'll avouch it.

La-CASTRE
You say well, Sir.

LUGIER
I know what I say, Sir, and I say but right, Sir;
I am no Trumpet of their Commendations
Before their Father; else I should say farther.

La-CASTRE
'Pray ye, what's this Gentleman?

NATOLET
One that lives with me, Sir;
A man well bred and learn'd, but blunt and bitter,
Yet it offends no wise man; I take pleasure in't:
Many fair gifts he has, in some of which
That lye most easie to their understandings,
H'as handsomely bred up my Girls, I thank him.
I have put it to 'em, that's my part, I have urg'd it,
It seems they are of years now to take hold on't.
He's wondrous blunt.

La-CASTRE
By my faith I was afraid of him:
Does he not fall out with the Gentlewomen sometimes?

NATOLET
No, no, he's that way moderate, and discreet, Sir.

ROSALURA
If he did, we should be too hard for him.

LUGIER
Well said Sulphur:
Too hard for thy Husbands head if he wear not armour.

[Enter **MIRABELL**, **PINAC**, **De-GARD**, **BELLEUR** and **ORIANA**.

NATOLET
Many of these bickrings, Sir.

La-CASTRE

I am glad they are no Oracles;
Sure, as I live, he beats them, he's so puisant.

ORIANA
Well, if ye do forget—

MIRABELL
Prithee hold thy peace;
I know thou art a pretty wench; I know thou lov'st me,
Preserve it till we have a fit time to discourse on't,
And a fit place: I'll ease thy heart I warrant thee:
Thou seest I have much to do now.

ORIANA
I am answer'd, Sir:
With me ye shall have nothing on these conditions.

De-GARD
Your Father and your friends.

La-CASTRE
You are welcome home, Sir;
'Bless ye, ye are very welcome:
'Pray know this Gentleman,
And these fair Ladies.

NATOLET
Monsieur Mirabell,
I am much affected with your fair return, Sir;
You bring a general joy.

MIRABELL
I bring you service,
And these bright Beauties, Sir.

NATOLET
Welcome home, Gentlemen,
Welcome, with all my heart.

BELLEUR
PINAC
We thank ye, Sir.

La-CASTRE
Your friends will have their share too.

BELLEUR
Sir, we hope

They'll look upon us, though we shew like strangers.

NATOLET

Monsieur De-Gard, I must salute you also,
And this fair Gentlewoman: you are welcome from your Travel too.
All welcome, all.

De-GARD

We render ye our loves, Sir:
The best Wealth we bring home: By your Favours, Beauties,
One of these two: you know my meaning.

ORIANA

Well, Sir:
They are fair and handsom, I must needs confess it;
And let it prove the worst, I shall live after it,
Whilst I have meat and drink Love cannot starve me;
For if I dye o'th' first fit I am unhappy,
And worthy to be buried with my heels upward.

MIRABELL

To marry, Sir?

La-CASTRE

You know I am an old man,
And every hour declining to my Grave,
One foot already in, more Sons I have not,
Nor more I dare not seek whilst you are worthy,
In you lies all my hope, and all my name,
The making good or wretched of my memory,
The safety of my state.

MIRABELL

And you have provided
Out of this tenderness these handsom Gentlewomen,
Daughters to this rich man, to take my choice of?

La-CASTRE

I have, dear Son.

MIRABELL

'Tis true, ye are old, and feebled;
Would ye were young again, and in full vigor;
I love a bounteous Fathers life, a long one,
I am none of those that when they shoot to ripeness,
Do what they can to break the boughs they grew on;
I wish ye many years and many Riches,
And pleasures to enjoy 'em: But for Marriage,

I neither yet believe in't, nor affect it,
Nor think it fit.

La-CASTRE
You will render me your reasons?

MIRABELL
Yes, Sir, both short and pithy, and these they are:
You would have me marry a Maid?

La-CASTRE
A Maid? what else?

MIRABELL
Yes, there be things called Widows, dead mens Wills,
I never lov'd to prove those; nor never long'd yet
To be buried alive in another mans cold monument.
And there be maids appearing, and maids being:
The appearing are fantastick things, meer shadows;
And if you mark 'em well, they want their heads too;
Only the World to cozen misty eyes,
Has clapt 'em on new faces. The maids being,
A man may venture on, if he be so mad to marry;
If he have neither fear before his eyes, nor fortune;
And let him take heed how he gathers these too,
For look ye, father, they are just like melons,
Musk-melons are the emblems of these maids;
Now they are ripe, now cut 'em, they taste pleasantly,
And are a dainty fruit, digested easily:
Neglect this present time, and come to morrow,
They are so ripe they are rotten gone, their sweetness
Run into humour, and their taste to surfeit.

La-CASTRE
Why, these are now ripe, Son.

MIRABELL
I'll try them presently,
And if I like their taste—

La-CASTRE
'Pray ye please your self, Sir.

MIRABELL
That liberty is my due, and I'll maintain it:
Lady, what think you of a handsom man now?

ROSALURA

A wholsom too, Sir.

MIRABELL
That's as you make your Bargain.
A handsom, wholsom man then, and a kind man,
To cheer your heart up, to rejoyce you, Lady?

ROSALURA
Yes Sir, I love rejoycing.

MIRABELL
To lye close to you?
Close as a Cockle? keep the cold nights from you?

ROSALURA
That will be lookt for too, our bodies ask it.

MIRABELL
And get two Boys at every Birth?

ROSALURA
That's nothing,
I have known a Cobler do it, a poor thin Cobler;
A Cobler out of mouldy Cheese perform it,
Cabbage, and coarse black Bread; methinks a Gentleman
Should take foul scorn to have an awl outname him.
Two at a Birth? why, every house-Dove has it:
That man that feeds well, promises as well too,
I should expect indeed something of worth from.
Ye talk of two?

MIRABELL
She would have me get two dozen,
Like Buttons, at a Birth.

ROSALURA
You love to brag, Sir.
If you proclaim these offers at your Marriage,
You are a pretty timber'd man, take heed.
They may be taken hold of, and expected,
Yes, if not hoped for at a higher rate too.

MIRABELL
I will take heed, and thank ye for your counsel:
Father, what think you?

La-CASTRE
'Tis a merry Gentlewoman;

Will make, no doubt, a good wife.

MIRABELL
Not for me:
I marry her, and happily get nothing;
In what a state am I then? Father, I shall suffer
For any thing I hear to the contrary, more majorum,
I were as sure to be a Cuckold, Father,
A Gentleman of Antler.

La-CASTRE
Away, away, fool.

MIRABELL
As I am sure to fail her expectation,
I had rather get the Pox than get her Babies.

La-CASTRE
Ye are much to blame; if this do not affect ye,
'Pray try the other; she's of a more demure way.

BELLEUR
That I had but the audacity to talk thus!
I love that plain-spoken Gentlewoman admirably,
And certain I could go as near to please her,
If down-right doing—she has a per'lous Countenance,
If I could meet one that would believe me,
And take my honest meaning without circumstance.

MIRABELL
You shall have your will, Sir, I will try the other,
But 'twill be to small use. I hope, fair Lady
(For methinks in your eyes I see more mercy)
You will enjoin your Lover a less penance;
And though I'll promise much, as men are liberal,
And vow an ample sacrifice of service,
Yet your discretion, and your tenderness,
And thriftiness in Love, good huswives carefulness
To keep the stock entire—

LILLIA-BIANCA
Good Sir, speak louder,
That these may witness too ye talk of nothing,
I should be loth alone to bear the burthen
Of so much indiscretion.

MIRABELL
Hark ye, hark ye;

Ods bobs, you are angry, Lady.

LILLIA-BIANCA
Angry? no, Sir;
I never own'd an anger to lose poorly.

MIRABELL
But you can love for all this, and delight too,
For all your set-austerity, to hear
Of a good husband, Lady?

LILLIA-BIANCA
You say true, Sir:
For by my troth, I have heard of none these ten years,
They are so rare, and there are so many, Sir,
So many longing-women on their knees too,
That pray the dropping down of these good husbands,
The droping down from heaven; for they are not bred here,
That you may guess at all my hope, but hearing—

MIRABELL
Why may not I be one?

LILLIA-BIANCA
You were near 'em once, Sir,
When ye came over the Alpes; those are near Heaven;
But since ye miss'd that happiness, there is no hope of ye.

MIRABELL
Can ye love a man?

LILLIA-BIANCA
Yes, if the man be lovely;
That is, be honest, modest; I would have him valiant,
His anger slow, but certain for his honour;
Travell'd he should be, but through himself exactly;
For 'tis fairer to know manners well than Countries;
He must be no vain Talker, nor no Lover
To hear himself talk, they are brags of a wanderer,
Of one finds no retreict for fair behaviour;
Would ye learn more?

MIRABELL
Yes.

LILLIA-BIANCA
Learn to hold your peace then,
Fond Girls are got with tongues, women with tempers.

MIRABELL

Women, with I know what; but let this vanish:
Go thy way good Wife Bias; sure thy Husband
Must have a strong Philosophers stone, he will ne'r please thee else.
Here's a starcht piece of austerity; do you hear, Father?
Do you hear this moral Lecture?

La-CASTRE

Yes, and like it.

MIRABELL

Why, there's your judgment now; there's an old bolt shot:
This thing must have the strangest observation,
Do you mark me (father?) when she is married once,
The strangest custom too of admiration
On all she does and speaks, 'twill be past sufferance;
I must not lie with her in common language,
Nor cry have at thee, Kate, I shall be hiss'd then;
Nor eat my meat without the sawce of sentences,
Your powder'd Beef, and Problems, a rare diet;
My first Son, Monsieur Aristotle, I know it,
Great Master of the Metaphysicks, or so;
The second Solon, and the best Law-setter;
And I must look Egyptian God-fathers,
Which will be no small trouble: my eldest daughter
Sapho, or such a fidling kind of Poetess,
And brought up, invita Minerva, at her needle.
My dogs must look their names too, and all Spartan,
Lelaps, Melampus; no more Fox and Baudiface.
I married to a sullen set of sentences?
To one that weighs her words and her behaviours
In the gold-weights of discretion? I'll be hang'd first.

La-CASTRE

Prithee reclaim thy self.

MIRABELL

'Pray ye give me time then;
If they can set me any thing to play at,
That seems fit for a Gamester, have at the fairest
Till I see more, and try more.

La-CASTRE

Take your time then,
I'll bar ye no fair liberty: come Gentlemen,
And Ladies come: to all once more welcome,
And now let's in to supper.

MIRABELL
How dost' like 'em?

PINAC
They are fair enough, but of so strange behaviours.

MIRABELL
Too strange for me; I must have those have mettle,
And mettle to my mind; Come, let's be merry.

BELLEUR
'Bless me from this woman: I would stand the Cannon
Before ten words of hers.

De GARD
Do you find him now?
Do you think he will be ever firm?

ORIANA
I fear not.

[Exeunt.

ACTUS SECUNDUS

SCÆNA PRIMA

Enter **MIRABELL, PINAC, BELLEUR.**

MIRABELL
Ne'r tell me of this happiness, 'tis nothing;
The state they bring with being sought to scurvey,
I had rather make mine own play, and I will do.
My happiness is in mine own content,
And the despising of such glorious trifles,
As I have done a thousand more. For my humour,
Give me a good free fellow, that sticks to me,
A jovial fair Companion; there's a Beauty:
For women, I can have too many of them;
Good women too, as the Age reckons 'em,
More than I have employment for.

PINAC
You are happy.

MIRABELL

My only fear is, that I must be forced
Against my nature, to conceal my self.
Health, and an able Body are two jewels.

PINAC

If either of these two women were offered to me now,
I would think otherwise, and do accordingly:
Yes, and recant my heresies, I would fain, Sir;
And be more tender of opinion,
And put a little off my travel'd liberty
Out of the way, and look upon 'em seriously.
Methinks this grave carried wench.

BELLEUR

Methinks the other,
The home-spoken Gentlewoman, that desires to be fruitful,
That treats of the full manage of the matter,
For there lies all my aim; that wench, methinks
If I were but well set on; for she is a fable,
If I were but hounded right, and one to teach me:
She speaks to th' matter, and comes home to th' point:
Now do I know I have such a body to please her,
As all the Kingdom cannot fit her with, I am sure on't,
If I could but talk my self into her favour.

MIRABELL

That's easily done.

BELLEUR

That's easily said, would 'twere done;
You should see then how I would lay about me;
If I were vertuous, it would never grieve me,
Or any thing that might justifie my modesty,
But when my nature is prone to do a charitie,
And my calfs-tongue will not help me.

MIRABELL

Will ye go to 'em?
They cannot but take it courteously.

PINAC

I'le do my part,
Though I am sure 'twill be the hardest I e're plaid yet,
A way I never try'd too, which will stagger me,
And if it do not shame me, I am happy.

MIRABELL

Win 'em, and wear 'em, I give up my interest.

PINAC
What say ye, Monsieur Bellure?

BELLEUR
Would I could say,
Or sing, or any thing that were but handsom,
I would be with her presently.

PINAC
Yours is no venture;
A merry ready wench.

BELLEUR
A vengeance squibber;
She'l fleer me out of faith too.

MIRABELL
I'le be near thee;
Pluck up thy heart, I'le second thee at all brunts;
Be angry if she abuse thee, and beat her a little,
Some women are won that way.

BELLEUR
Pray be quiet,
And let me think: I am resolv'd to go on;
But how I shall get off again—

MIRABELL
I am perswaded
Thou wilt so please her, she will go near to ravish thee.

BELLEUR
I would 'twere come to that once: let me pray a little.

MIRABELL
Now for thine honour Pinac; board me this modesty,
Warm but this frozen snow-ball, 'twill be a conquest
(Although I know thou art a fortunate Wencher,
And hast done rarely in thy daies) above all thy ventures.

BELLEUR
You will be ever near?

MIRABELL
At all necessities,
And take thee off, and set thee on again, Boy;

And cherish thee, and stroak thee.

BELLEUR
Help me out too?
For I know I shall stick i'th' mire: if ye see us close once,
Be gone, and leave me to my fortune, suddenly,
For I am then determin'd to do wonders.
Farewel, and fling an old shooe: how my heart throbs!
Would I were drunk: Farewel Pinac; Heaven send us
A joyfull and a merry meeting, man.

PINAC
Farewel,
And chear thy heart up; and remember Bellure
They are but women.

BELLEUR
I had rather they were Lyons.

[Exeunt.

MIRABELL
About it; I'le be with you instantly.

[Enter **ORIANA**.

Shall I ne'r be at rest? no peace of conscience?
No quiet for these creatures? Am I ordain'd
To be devour'd quick by these she-Canibals?
Here's another they call handsom, I care not for her,
I ne'r look after her: when I am half tipled
It may be I should turn her, and peruse her,
Or in my want of women, I might call for her;
But to be haunted when I have no fancie,
No maw to th' matter—Now, why do you follow me?

ORIANA
I hope, Sir, 'tis no blemish to my vertue,
Nor need you (out of scruple) ask that question,
If you remember ye, before your Travel
The contract you ty'd to me: 'tis my love, Sir,
That makes me seek ye, to confirm your memory,
And that being fair and good, I cannot suffer:
I come to give ye thanks too.

MIRABELL
For what 'prethee?

ORIANA

For that fair piece of honesty ye shew'd, Sir,
That constant nobleness.

MIRABELL

How? for I am short headed.

ORIANA

I'le tell ye then; for refusing that free offer
Of Monsieur Natolets; those handsom Beauties,
Those two prime Ladies, that might well have prest ye,
If not to have broken, yet to have bow'd your promise,
I know it was for my sake, for your faith sake,
You slipt 'em off: your honesty compell'd ye.
And let me tell ye, Sir, it shew'd most handsomly.

MIRABELL

And let me tell thee, there was no such matter:
Nothing intended that way of that nature;
I have more to do with my honesty than to fool it,
Or venture it in such leak barks as women;
I put 'em off, because I lov'd 'em not,
Because they are too queazie for my temper,
And not for thy sake, nor the Contract sake,
Nor vows, nor oaths; I have made a thousand of 'em,
They are things indifferent, whether kept or broken;
Meer venial slips, that grow not near the conscience;
Nothing concerns those tender parts; they are trifles;
For, as I think, there was never man yet hop'd for
Either constancie, or secrecie, from a woman,
Unless it were an Ass ordain'd for sufferance;
Nor to contract with such can be a Tial;
So let them know again; for 'tis a Justice,
And a main point of civil policie,
What e're we say or swear, they being Reprobates,
Out of the state of faith, we are clear of all sides,
And 'tis a curious blindness to believe us.

ORIANA

You do not mean this sure?

MIRABELL

Yes sure, and certain,
And hold it positively, as a Principle,
As ye are strange things, and made of strange fires and fluxes,
So we are allow'd as strange wayes to obtain ye,
But not to hold; we are all created Errant.

ORIANA

You told me other tales.

MIRABELL

I not deny it;
I have tales of all sorts for all sorts of women,
And protestations likewise of all sizes,
As they have vanities to make us coxcombs;
If I obtain a good turn, so it is,
I am thankfull for it: if I be made an Ass,
The mends are in mine own hands, or the Surgeons,
And there's an end on't.

ORIANA

Do not you love me then?

MIRABELL

As I love others, heartily I love thee,
When I am high and lusty, I love thee cruelly:
After I have made a plenteous meal, and satisfi'd
My senses with all delicates, come to me,
And thou shalt see how I love thee.

ORIANA

Will not you marry me?

MIRABELL

No, certain, no, for any thing I know yet;
I must not lose my liberty, dear Lady,
And like a wanton slave cry for more shackles.
What should I marry for? Do I want any thing?
Am I an inch the farther from my pleasure?
Why should I be at charge to keep a wife of mine own,
When other honest married men will ease me?
And thank me too, and be beholding to me:
Thou thinkst I am mad for a Maiden-head, thou art cozen'd;
Or if I were addicted to that diet
Can you tell me where I should have one? thou art eighteen now,
And if thou hast thy Maiden-head yet extant,
Sure 'tis as big as Cods-head: and those grave dishes
I never love to deal withal: Do'st thou see this book here?
Look over all these ranks; all these are women,
Maids, and pretenders to Maiden-heads; these are my conquests,
All these I swore to marry, as I swore to thee,
With the same reservation, and most righteously,
Which I need not have done neither; for alas they made no scruple,
And I enjoy'd 'em at my will, and left 'em:
Some of 'em are married since, and were as pure maids again,

Nay o' my conscience better than they were bred for;
The rest fine sober women.

ORIANA
Are ye not asham'd, Sir?

MIRABELL
No by my troth, Sir; there's no shame belongs to it;
I hold it as commendable to be wealthy in pleasure,
As others do in rotten sheep, and pasture.

[Enter **De GARD**.

ORIANA
Are all my hopes come to this? is there no faith?
No troth? nor modesty in men?

De GARD
How now Sister,
Why weeping thus? did I not prophesie?
Come tell me why—

ORIANA
I am not well; 'pray ye pardon me.

[Exit.

De GARD
Now Monsieur Mirabel, what ails my Sister?
You have been playing the wag with her.

MIRABELL
As I take it,
She is crying for a cod-piece; is she gone?
Lord, what an Age is this! I was calling for ye,
For as I live I thought she would have ravish'd me.

De GARD
Ye are merry Sir.

MIRABELL
Thou know'st this book, de Gard, this Inventory.

De GARD
The debt-book of your Mistresses, I remember it.

MIRABELL
Why this was it that anger'd her; she was stark mad

She found not her name here, and cry'd down-right,
Because I would not pity her immediately,
And put her in my list.

De GARD
Sure she had more modesty.

MIRABELL
Their modesty is anger to be over-done;
They'l quarrel sooner for precedence here,
And take it in more dudgeon to be slighted,
Than they will in publique meetings; 'tis their natures:
And alas I have so many to dispatch yet,
And to provide my self for my affairs too,
That in good faith—

De GARD
Be not too glorious foolish;
Summe not your Travels up with vanities,
It ill becomes your expectation:
Temper your speech, Sir; whether your loose story
Be true, or false (for you are so free, I fear it)
Name not my Sister in't; I must not hear it;
Upon your danger name her not: I hold her
A Gentlewoman of those happy parts and carriage,
A good mans tongue may be right proud to speak her.

MIRABELL
Your Sister, Sir? d'ye blench at that? d'ye cavil?
Do you hold her such a piece, she may not be play'd withal?
I have had an hundred handsomer and nobler,
Have su'd to me too for such a courtesie:
Your Sister comes i'th' rear: since ye are so angry,
And hold your Sister such a strong Recusant,
I tell ye I may do it, and it may be will too,
It may be have too, there's my free confession;
Work upon that now.

De GARD
If I thought ye had, I would work,
And work such stubborn work, should make your heart ake;
But I believe ye, as I ever knew ye,
A glorious talker, and a Legend maker
Of idle tales, and trifles; a depraver
Of your own truth; their honours fly about ye;
And so I take my leave, but with this caution,
Your sword be surer than your tongue, you'l smart else.

MIRABELL

I laugh at thee, so little I respect thee;
And I'le talk louder, and despise thy Sister;
Set up a Chamber-maid that shall out-shine her,
And carry her in my Coach too, and that will kill her.
Go get thy Rents up, go.

De GARD

Ye are a fine Gentleman.

[Exit.

MIRABELL

Now have at my two youths, I'le see how they do,
How they behave themselves, and then I'le study
What wench shall love me next, and when I'le lose her.

[Exit.

SCÆNA SECUNDA

Enter **PINAC** and a **SERVANT**.

PINAC

Art thou her servant, saist thou?

SERVANT

Her poor creature,
But servant to her horse, Sir.

PINAC

Canst thou shew me
The way to her chamber? or where I may conveniently
See her, or come to talk to her?

SERVANT

That I can, Sir;
But the question is whether I will or no.

PINAC

Why I'le content thee.

SERVANT

Why I'le content thee then; now ye come to me.

PINAC

There's for your diligence.

SERVANT
There's her chamber, Sir;
And this way she comes out; stand ye but here, Sir,
You have her at your prospect, or your pleasure.

PINAC
Is she not very angry?

SERVANT
You'l find that quickly:
May be she'll call ye sawcy scurvey fellow,
Or some such familiar name: 'may be she knows ye,
And will fling a Piss-pot at ye, or a Pantofle,
According as ye are in acquaintance: if she like ye,
'May be she'll look upon ye, 'may be no,
And two moneths hence call for ye.

PINAC
This is fine.
She is monstrous proud then?

SERVANT
She is a little haughtie;
Of a small body, she has a mind well mounted.
Can ye speak Greek?

PINAC
No, certain.

SERVANT
Get ye gone then;
And talk of stars, and firmaments, and fire-drakes.
Do you remember who was Adams School-master,
And who taught Eve to spin? she knows all these,
And will run ye over the beginning o'th' world
As familiar as a Fidler.
Can ye sit seven hours together, and say nothing?
Which she will do, and when she speaks, speak Oracles;
Speak things that no man understands, nor her self neither.

PINAC
Thou mak'st me wonder.

SERVANT
Can ye smile?

PINAC

Yes willingly:

For naturally I bear a mirth about me.

SERVANT

She'l ne'r endure ye then; she is never merry;

If she see one laugh, she'll swound past Aqua vitæ:

Never come near her, Sir; if ye chance to venture,

And talk not like a Doctor, you are damn'd too;

I have told enough for your crown, and so good speed ye.

[Exit.

PINAC

I have a pretty task, if she be thus curious,

As sure it seems she is; if I fall off now,

I shall be laugh'd at fearfully; if I go forward,

I can but be abus'd, and that I look for,

And yet I may hit right, but 'tis unlikely.

Stay, in what mood and figure shall I attempt her?

A careless way? no, no, that will not waken her;

Besides, her gravity will give me line still,

And let me lose my self; yet this way often

Has hit, and handsomly. A wanton method?

I, if she give it leave to sink into her consideration;

But there's the doubt: if it but stir her blood once,

And creep into the crannies of her phansie,

Set her a gog: but if she chance to slight it,

And by the pow'r of her modesty fling it back,

I shall appear the arrantst Rascal to her,

The most licentious knave, for I shall talk lewdly.

To bear my self austerely? rate my words,

And fling a general gravitie about me,

As if I meant to give Laws? but this I cannot do,

This is a way above my understanding;

Or if I could, 'tis odds she'll think I mock her;

For serious and sad things are ever still suspicious.

Well, I'le say something.

But learning I have none, and less good manners,

Especially for Ladies; well, I'le set my best face;

[Enter **LILLIA-BIANCA**, **PETELLA**

I hear some coming; this is the first woman

I ever fear'd yet, the first face that shakes me,

LILLIA-BIANCA

Give me my hat Petella, take this veil off,

This sullen cloud, it darkens my delights;
Come wench be free, and let the Musick warble,
Play me some lusty measure.

PINAC
This is she sure,
The very same I saw, the very woman,
The Gravitie I wonder'd at: Stay, stay,
Let me be sure; ne'r trust me, but she danceth,
Summer is in her face now, and she skippeth:
I'le go a little nearer.

LILLIA-BIANCA
Quicker time fellows,

[Enter **MIRABELL**.

I cannot find my legs yet, now Petella.

PINAC
I am amaz'd, I am founder'd in my fancies.

MIRABELL
Hah, say ye so; is this your gravitie?
This the austeritie ye put upon ye?
I'le see more o' this sport.

LILLIA-BIANCA
A Song now;
Call in for a merry, and a light Song,
And sing it with a liberal spirit.

[Enter a **MAN**.

MAN
Yes, Madam.

LILLIA-BIANCA
And be not amaz'd Sirrah, but take us for your own company.
Let's walk our selves: come wench, would we had a man or two.

PINAC
Sure she has spi'd me, and will abuse me dreadfully,
She has put on this for the purpose; yet I will try her.
Madam, I would be loth my rude intrusion,
Which I must crave a pardon for—

LILLIA-BIANCA

O ye are welcom,
Ye are very welcom, Sir, we want such a one;
Strike up again: I dare presume ye dance well:
Quick, quick, Sir, quick, the time steals on.

PINAC
I would talk with ye.

LILLIA-BIANCA
Talk as ye dance.

MIRABELL
She'l beat him off his legs first,
This is the finest Masque.

LILLIA-BIANCA
Now how do ye, Sir?

PINAC
You have given me a shrewd heat.

LILLIA-BIANCA
I'le give ye a hundred.
Come sing now, sing; for I know ye sing well,
I see ye have a singing face.

PINAC
A fine Modesty!
If I could, she'd never give me breath,
Madam would I might sit and recover.

LILLIA-BIANCA
Sit here, and sing now,
Let's do things quickly, Sir, and handsomly,
Sit close wench, close, begin, begin.

[SONG.

PINAC
I am lesson'd.

LILLIA-BIANCA
'Tis very pretty i'faith, give me some wine now.

PINAC
I would fain speak to ye.

LILLIA-BIANCA

You shall drink first, believe me:
Here's to ye a lusty health.

PINAC
I thank ye Lady,
Would I were off again; I smell my misery;
I was never put to this rack; I shall be drunk too.

MIRABELL
If thou be'st not a right one, I have lost mine aim much:
I thank Heaven that I have scap'd thee; To her Pinac;
For thou art as sure to have her, and to groan for her—
I'le see how my other youth does; this speeds trimly:
A fine grave Gentlewoman, and worth much honour.

[Exit.

LILLIA-BIANCA
Now? how do ye like me, Sir?

PINAC
I like ye rarely.

LILLIA-BIANCA
Ye see, Sir, though sometimes we are grave and silent,
And put on sadder dispositions,
Yet we are compounded of free parts, and sometimes too
Our lighter, airie, and our fierie mettles
Break out, and shew themselves; and what think you of that Sir?

PINAC
Good Lady sit, for I am very weary;
And then I'le tell ye.

LILLIA-BIANCA
Fie, a young man idle?
Up, and walk; be still in action.
The motions of the body are fair beauties,
Besides 'tis cold; ods-me Sir, let's walk faster,
What think ye now of the Lady Felicia?
And Bella-fronte the Dukes fair Daughter? ha?
Are they not handsom things? there is Duarta,
And brown Olivia.

PINAC
I know none of 'em.

LILLIA-BIANCA

But brown must not be cast away, Sir; if young Lelia
Had kept her self till this day from a Husband,
Why what a Beauty, Sir! you know Ismena
The fair Jem of Saint Germans?

PINAC
By my troth I do not.

LILLIA-BIANCA
And then I know you must hear of Brisac,
How unlike a Gentleman—

PINAC
As I live I have heard nothing.

LILLIA-BIANCA
Strike me another Galliard.

PINAC
By this light I cannot;
In troth I have sprain'd my leg, Madam.

LILLIA-BIANCA
Now sit ye down, Sir,
And tell me why ye came hither, why ye chose me out?
What is your business? your errant? dispatch, dispatch!
'May be ye are some Gentlemans man, and I mistook ye,
That have brought me a Letter, or a haunch of Venison,
Sent me from some friend of mine.

PINAC
Do I look like a Carrier?
You might allow me what I am, a Gentleman.

LILLIA-BIANCA
Cry 'ye mercie, Sir, I saw ye yesterday,
You are new come out of Travel, I mistook ye;
And how do all our impudent friends in Italie?

PINAC
Madam, I came with duty, and fair courtesie,
Service, and honour to ye.

LILLIA-BIANCA
Ye came to jear me:
Ye see I am merry, Sir, I have chang'd my copy:
None of the Sages now, and 'pray ye proclaim it,
Fling on me what aspersion you shall please, Sir,

Of wantonness, or wildness, I look for it;
And tell the world I am an hypocrite,
Mask in a forc'd and borrow'd shape, I expect it;
But not to have you believ'd; for mark ye, Sir,
I have won a nobler estimation,
A stronger tie by my discretion
Upon opinion (how e're you think I forced it)
Than either tongue or art of yours can slubber,
And when I please I will be what I please, Sir,
So I exceed not Mean; and none shall brand it
Either with scorn or shame, but shall be slighted.

PINAC
Lady, I come to love ye.

LILLIA-BIANCA
Love your self, Sir,
And when I want observers, I'll send for ye:
Heigh, ho; my fit's almost off, for we do all by fits, Sir:
If ye be weary, sit till I come again to ye.

[Exit.

PINAC
This is a wench of a dainty spirit; but hang me if I know yet
Either what to think, or make of her; she had her will of me,
And baited me abundantly, I thank her,
And I confess I never was so blurted,
Nor ever so abus'd; I must bear mine own sins;
Ye talk of Travels, here's a curious Country,
Yet I will find her out, or forswear my facultie.

[Exit.

Enter **ROSALURA** and **ORIANA**.

ROSALURA
Ne'r vex your self, nor grieve; ye are a fool then.

ORIANA
I am sure I am made so: yet before I suffer
Thus like a girl, and give him leave to triumph—

ROSALURA

You say right; for as long as he perceives ye
Sink under his proud scornings, he'll laugh at ye:
For me secure your self; and for my Sister,
I partly know her mind too: howsoever
To obey my Father we have made a tender
Of our poor beauties to the travel'd Monsieur;
Yet two words to a bargain; he slights us
As skittish things, and we shun him as curious.
May be my free behaviour turns his stomach,
And makes him seem to doubt a loose opinion.
I must be so sometimes, though all the world saw it.

ORIANA
Why should not ye? Are our minds only measur'd?
As long as here ye stand secure.

ROSALURA
Ye say true;
As long as mine own Conscience makes no question,
What care I for Report? That Woman's miserable
That's good or bad for their tongues sake: Come let's retire.
And get my veil Wench: By my troth your sorrow,
And the consideration of mens humorous maddings,
Have put me into a serious contemplation.

[Enter **MIRABELL** and **BELLEUR**.

ORIANA
Come 'faith, let's sit, and think.

ROSALURA
That's all my business.

MIRABELL
Why standst thou peeping here? thou great slug, forward.

BELLEUR
She is there, peace.

MIRABELL
Why standst thou here then,
Sneaking, and peaking, as thou would'st steal linnen?
Hast thou not place and time?

BELLEUR
I had a rare speech
Studied, and almost ready, and your violence
Has beat it out of my brains.

MIRABELL

Hang your rare speeches,
Go me on like a man.

BELLEUR

Let me set my Beard up.
How has Pinac performed?

MIRABELL

He has won already:
He stands not thrumming of caps thus.

BELLEUR

Lord, what should I ail?
What a cold I have over my stomach; would I had some Hum.
Certain I have a great mind to be at her:
A mighty mind.

MIRABELL

On fool.

BELLEUR

Good words, I beseech ye;
For I will not be abused by both.

MIRABELL

Adieu, then,
I will not trouble you, I see you are valiant,
And work your own way.

BELLEUR

Hist, hist, I will be rul'd,
I will 'faith, I will go presently:
Will ye forsake me now and leave me i'th' suds?
You know I am false-hearted this way; I beseech ye,
Good sweet Mirabel; I'le cut your throat if ye leave me,
Indeed I will sweet heart.

MIRABELL

I will be ready,
Still at thine elbow; take a mans heart to thee,
And speak thy mind: the plainer still the better.
She is a woman of that free behaviour,
Indeed that common courtesie, she cannot deny thee;
Go bravely on.

BELLEUR

Madam—keep close about me,
Still at my back. Madam, sweet Madam—

ROSALURA
Ha;
What noise is that, what saucy sound to trouble me?

MIRABELL
What said she?

BELLEUR
I am saucy.

MIRABELL
'Tis the better.

BELLEUR
She comes; must I be saucy still?

MIRABELL
More saucy.

ROSALURA
Still troubled with these vanities? Heaven bless us;
What are we born to? would ye speak with any of my people?
Go in, Sir, I am busie.

BELLEUR
This is not she sure:
Is this two Children at a Birth? I'le be hang'd then:
Mine was a merry Gentlewoman, talkt daintily,
Talkt of those matters that befitted women;
This is a parcel-pray'r-book; I'm serv'd sweetly;
And now I am to look too; I was prepar'd for th' other way.

ROSALURA
Do you know that man?

ORIANA
Sure I have seen him, Lady.

ROSALURA
Methinks 'tis pity such a lusty fellow
Should wander up and down and want employment.

BELLEUR
She takes me for a Rogue: you may do well, Madam,
To stay this wanderer, and set him a work, forsooth,

He can do something that may please your Ladiship.
I have heard of Women that desire good breedings,
Two at a birth, or so.

ROSALURA
The fellow's impudent.

ORIANA
Sure he is crazed.

ROSALURA
I have heard of men too, that have had good manners;
Sure this is want of grace; indeed 'tis great pity
The young man has been bred so ill; but this lewd Age
Is full of such examples.

BELLEUR
I am founder'd,
And some shall rue the setting of me on.

MIRABELL
Ha? so bookish, Lady, is it possible?
Turn'd holy at the heart too? I'le be hang'd then:
Why this is such a feat, such an activity,
Such fast and loose: a veyl too for your Knavery?
O dio, dio!

ROSALURA
What do you take me for, Sir?

MIRABELL
An hypocrite, a wanton, a dissembler,
How e're ye seem, and thus ye are to be handled.
Mark me Belleur, and this you love, I know it.

ROSALURA
Stand off, bold Sir.

MIRABELL
You wear good Cloaths to this end,
Jewels, love Feasts, and Masques.

ROSALURA
Ye are monstrous saucy.

MIRABELL
All this to draw on fools? and thus, thus Lady,
Ye are to be lull'd.

BELLEUR

Let her alone, I'le swinge ye else,
I will 'faith; for though I cannot skill o'this matter
My self, I will not see another do it before me,
And do it worse.

ROSALURA

Away, ye are a vain thing;
You have travell'd far, Sir, to return again
A windy and poor Bladder: you talk of Women,
That are not worth the favour of a common one;
The grace of her grew in an Hospital:
Against a thousand such blown fooleries
I am able to maintain good Womens honours,
Their freedoms, and their fames, and I will do it.

MIRABELL

She has almost struck me dumb too.

ROSALURA

And declaim
Against your base malicious tongues; your noises;
For they are nothing else: You teach behaviours?
Or touch us for our freedoms? teach your selves manners,
Truth and sobriety, and live so clearly
That our lives may shine in ye; and then task us:
It seems ye are hot, the suburbs will supply ye.
Good Women scorn such Gamesters; so I'le leave ye,
I am sorry to see this: 'faith Sir, live fairly.

[Exit.

MIRABELL

This woman, if she hold on, may be vertuous,
'Tis almost possible: we'll have a new day.

BELLEUR

Ye brought me on, ye forced me to this foolery;
I am asham'd, I am scorn'd, I am flurted; yes, I am so:
Though I cannot talk to a woman like your worship,
And use my phrases, and my learned figures,
Yet I can fight with any man.

MIRABELL

Fie.

BELLEUR

I can, Sir,
And I will fight.

MIRABELL
With whom?

BELLEUR
With you, with any man;
For all men now will laugh at me.

MIRABELL
Prethee be moderate.

BELLEUR
And I'le beat all men. Come.

MIRABELL
I love thee dearly.

BELLEUR
I beat all that love, Love has undone me;
Never tell me, I will not be a History.

MIRABELL
Thou art not.

BELLEUR
'Sfoot I will not; give me room,
And let me see the proudest of ye jeer me,
And I'le begin with you first.

MIRABELL
'Prethee Belleur;
If I do not satisfie thee—

BELLEUR
Well, look ye do:
But now I think on't better, 'tis impossible;
I must beat some body, I am maul'd my self,
And I ought in justice—

MIRABELL
No, no, no, ye are couzen'd;
But walk, and let me talk to thee.

BELLEUR
Talk wisely,
And see that no man laugh upon no occasion;

For I shall think then 'tis at me.

MIRABELL
I warrant thee.

BELLEUR
Nor no more talk of this.

MIRABELL
Do'st think I am maddish?

BELLEUR
I must needs fight yet; for I find it concerns me,
A pox on't, I must fight.

MIRABELL
'Faith thou shalt not.

[Exeunt.

ACTUS TERTIUS

SCÆNA PRIMA

Enter **De GARD**, and Leverdure, alias **LUGIER**.

De GARD
I know ye are a Scholar, and can do wonders.

LUGIER
There's no great Scholarship belongs to this, Sir;
What I am, I am; I pity your poor Sister,
And heartily I hate these Travellers,
These Gim-cracks, made of Mops, and Motions:
There's nothing in their houses here but hummings;
A Bee has more brains. I grieve, and vex too
The insolent licentious carriage
Of this out-facing fellow, Mirabell,
And I am mad to see him prick his plumes up.

De GARD
His wrongs you partly know.

LUGIER
Do not you stir, Sir,
Since he has begun with wit, let wit revenge it;

Keep your sword close, we'll cut his throat a new way.
I am asham'd the Gentlewoman should suffer
Such base lewd wrongs.

De GARD

I will be rul'd, he shall live,
And left to your revenge.

LUGIER

I, I, I'le fit him:
He makes a common scorn of handsome Women;
Modesty, and good manners are his May-games:
He takes up Maidenheads with a new Commission;
The Church warrant's out of date: follow my Counsel,
For I am zealous in the Cause.

De GARD

I will, Sir;
And will be still directed: for the truth is
My Sword will make my Sister seem more monstrous:
Besides there is no honour won on Reprobates.

LUGIER

You are i'th' right: The slight he has shew'd my Pupils,
Sets me a fire too: go I'le prepare your Sister,
And as I told ye.

De GARD

Yes all shall be fit, Sir.

LUGIER

And seriously, and handsomely.

De GARD

I warrant ye.

LUGIER

A little counsel more.

De GARD

'Tis well.

LUGIER

Most stately.
See that observ'd; and then.

De GARD

I have ye every way.

LUGIER

Away then and be ready.

De GARD

With all speed, Sir.

[Exit.

[Enter **LILLIA-BIANCA**, **ROSALURA** and **ORIANA**.

LUGIER

We'll learn to travel too, may be beyond him.
Good day, Fair beauties.

LILLIA-BIANCA

You have beautified us.
We thank ye, Sir, ye have set us off most gallantly
With your grave precepts.

ROSALURA

We expected Husbands
Out of your Documents, and taught behaviours;
Excellent Husbands, thought men would run stark mad on us,
Men of all Ages, and all states: we expected
An Inundation of desires, and offers,
A Torrent of trim Suitors: all we did,
Or said, or purpos'd to be Spells about us,
Spells to provoke—

LILLIA-BIANCA

Ye have provoke'd us finely,
We follow'd your directions, we did rarely,
We were Stately, Coy, Demure, Careless, Light, Giddy,
And play'd at all points: This you swore would carry.

ROSALURA

We made Love, and contemn'd Love. Now seem'd holy
With such a reverent put-on Reservation
Which could not miss according to your Principles,
Now gave more hope again. Now close, now publick,
Still up and down, we beat it like a Billow;
And ever those behaviours you read to us,
Subtil, and new. But all this will not help us.

LILLIA-BIANCA

They help to hinder us of all Acquaintance,
They have frighted off all Friends: what am I better

For all my Learning, if I love a Dunce,
A handsome dunce? to what use serves my Reading?
You should have taught me what belongs to Horses,
Doggs, Dice, Hawks, Banquets, Masks, free and fair Meetings,
To have studied Gowns and Dressings.

LUGIER
Ye are not mad sure.

ROSALURA
We shall be if we follow your encouragements;
I'le take mine own way now.

LILLIA-BIANCA
And I my fortune:
We may live Maids else till the Moon drop Mil-stones;
I see your modest Women are taken for monsters,
A Dowry of good breeding is worth nothing.

LUGIER
Since ye take it so to th' heart, pray'ye give me leave yet,
And ye shall see how I'le convert this Heretick;
Mark how this Mirabell—

LILLIA-BIANCA
Name him no more:
For, though I long for a Husband, I hate him,
And would be marryed sooner to a Monkey,
Or to a Jack of Straw, than such a Juggler.

ROSALURA
I am of that mind too; he is too nimble,
And plays at fast and loose too learnedly
For a plain-meaning Woman; that's the truth on't.
Here's one too, that we love well, would be angry;
And reason why: No, no, we will not trouble ye
Nor him, at this time: may he make you happy.
We'll turn our selves loose now, to our fair fortunes,
And the down-right way.

LILLIA-BIANCA
The winning-way we'll follow,
We'll bait, that men may bite fair, and not be frighted;
Yet we'll not be carryed so cheap neither: we'll have some sport,
Some mad-Morris or other for our mony, Tutor.

LUGIER
'Tis like enough: prosper your own Devices;

Ye are old enough to choose: But for this Gentlewoman,
So please her, give me leave.

ORIANA
I shall be glad, Sir,
To find a friend, whose pity may direct me.

LUGIER
I'le do my best, and faithfully deal for ye;
But then ye must be ruled.

ORIANA
In all, I vow to ye.

ROSALURA
Do, do: he has a lucky hand sometimes, I'le assure ye:
And hunts the recovery of a lost Lover deadly.

LUGIER
You must away straight.

ORIANA
Yes.

LUGIER
And I'le instruct ye:
Here ye can know no more.

ORIANA
By your leave, sweet Ladies,
And all our Fortunes, arrive at our own wishes.

LILLIA-BIANCA
Amen, Amen.

LUGIER
I must borrow your man.

LILLIA-BIANCA
'Pray take him;
He is within: to do her good, take any thing,
Take us, and all.

LUGIER
No doubt ye may find Takers;
And so we'll leave ye to your own disposes.

[Exeunt.

LILLIA-BIANCA

Now which way, Wench.

ROSALURA

We'll go a brave way; fear not:
A safe, and sure way too: and yet a by-way,
I must confess I have a great mind to be married.

LILLIA-BIANCA

So have I too, a grudging of good-will that way;
And would as fain be dispatch'd. But this Monsieur Quicksilver.

ROSALURA

No, no: we'll bar him, by, and Main: Let him trample;
There is no safety in his Surquedrie:
An Army-Royal of women, are too few for him,
He keeps a Journal of his Gentleness,
And will go near to print his fair dispatches,
And call it his triumph over time and women:
Let him pass out of memory: what think ye
Of his two Companions?

LILLIA-BIANCA

Pinac methinks is reasonable;
A little modestie he has brought home with him,
And might be taught in time some handsom duty.

ROSALURA

They say he is a wencher too.

LILLIA-BIANCA

I like him better:
A free light touch or two becomes a Gentleman,
And sets him seemly off: so he exceed not,
But keep his compass, clear he may be lookt at;
I would not marry a man that must be taught,
And conjur'd up with kisses; the best game
Is plaid still by the best Gamesters.

ROSALURA

Fie upon thee!
What talk hast thou?

LILLIA-BIANCA

Are not we alone, and merry?
Why should we be asham'd to speak what we think? thy Gentleman
The tall fat fellow; he that came to see thee.

ROSALURA

Is't not a goodly man?

LILLIA-BIANCA

A wondrous goodly!
H'as weight enough I warrant thee: Mercy upon me;
What a Serpent wilt thou seem under such a S. George.

ROSALURA

Thou art a fool; give me a man brings Mettle,
Brings substance with him; needs no Broths to Lare him:
These little fellows shew like Fleas in boxes,
Hop up and down, and keep a stir to vex us;
Give me the puissant Pike, take you the small shot.

LILLIA-BIANCA

Of a great thing I have not seen a duller,
Therefore methinks, sweet Sister—

ROSALURA

Peace: he's modest:
A bashfulness, which is a point of grace, wench:
But when these fellows come to moulding, Sister,
To heat, and handling: as I live, I like him;

[Enter **MIRABELL**.

And methinks I could form him.

LILLIA-BIANCA

Peace: the Fire-drake.

MIRABELL

'Bless ye sweet beauties: sweet incomparable Ladies:
Sweet wits: sweet humours: 'Bless you, learned Lady,
And you, most holy Nun; 'Bless your Devotions.

LILLIA-BIANCA

And 'bless your brains, Sir, your most pregnant brains, Sir,
They are in Travail, may they be delivered
Of a most hopeful Wild-Goose.

ROSALURA

'Bless your manhood:
They say ye are a Gentleman of action,
A fair accomplish'd man; and a rare Engineer,
You have a trick to blow up Maidenheads,

A subtle trick, they say abroad.

MIRABELL
I have Lady.

ROSALURA
And often glory in their Ruines.

MIRABELL
Yes forsooth;
I have a speedy trick: please you to try it:
My Engine will dispatch ye instantly.

ROSALURA
I would I were a woman, Sir, fit for ye,
As there be such, no doubt, may Engine you too;
May with a Counter-mine blow up your valour:
But in good faith, Sir, we are both too honest:
And the plague is, we can not be perswaded:
For, look ye: if we thought it were a glory
To be the last of all your lovely Ladies.

MIRABELL
Come, come; leave prating: this has spoil'd your Market;
This pride, and pufft-up heart, will make ye fast, Ladies,
Fast, when ye are hungry too.

ROSALURA
The more our pain, Sir.

LILLIA-BIANCA
The more our health, I hope too.

MIRABELL
Your behaviours
Have made men stand amaz'd; those men that lov'd ye;
Men of fair States and parts; your strange conventions
Into I know not what, nor how, nor wherefore;
Your scorns of those that came to visit ye;
Your studied Whim-whams; and your fine set faces:
What have these got ye? proud, and harsh opinions:
A Travel'd-Monsieur, was the strangest Creature,
The wildest Monster to be wondred at:
His Person made a publique Scoff, his knowledge,
(As if he had been bred 'mongst Bears or Bandoggs)
Shunn'd and avoided: his conversation snuft at.
What Harvest brings all this?

ROSALURA

I pray ye proceed, Sir.

MIRABELL

Now ye shall see in what esteem a Traveller,
An understanding Gentleman, and a Monsieur
Is to be held, and to your griefs confess it,
Both to your griefs, and galls.

LILLIA-BIANCA

In what I pray ye, Sir?
We would be glad to understand your excellence.

MIRABELL

Goe on, (sweet Ladies) it becomes ye rarely.
For me, I have blest me from ye, scoff on seriously,
And note the Man ye mock'd: you, (Lady Learning)
Note the poor Traveller, that came to visit ye,
That flat unfurnish'd fellow: note him throughly,
You may chance to see him anon.

LILLIA-BIANCA

'Tis very likely.

MIRABELL

And see him Courted by a Travell'd Lady,
Held dear, and honour'd by a vertuous virgin,
May be a Beautie, not far short of yours, neither
It may be, clearer.

LILLIA-BIANCA

Not unlikely.

MIRABELL

Younger:
As killing eyes as yours: a wit as poynant
May be, a State to that may top your Fortune;
Enquire how she thinks of him, how she holds him;
His good parts; in what precious price already;
Being a stranger to him, how she courts him;
A stranger to his Nation too, how she dotes on him:
Enquire of this; be sick to know: Curse, Lady,
And keep your chamber: cry, and curse: a sweet one,
A thousand in yearly land; well bred; well friended:
Travell'd, and highly followed for her fashions.

LILLIA-BIANCA

'Bless his good fortune, Sir.

MIRABELL
This scurvy fellow;
I think they call his name Pinac; this serving-man
That brought ye Venison, as I take it, Madam;
Note but this Scab; 'tis strange that this course creature,
That has no more set off, but his jugglings,
His travell'd tricks.

LILLIA-BIANCA
Good, Sir, I grieve not at him,
Nor envy not his fortune: yet I wonder,
He's handsom; yet I see no such perfection.

MIRABELL
Would I had his fortune: for 'tis a woman
Of that sweet temper'd nature, and that judgment,
Besides her state, that care, clear understanding,
And such a wife to bless him.

ROSALURA
Pray ye whence is she?

MIRABELL
Of England, and a most accomplish'd Lady,
So modest that mens eyes are frighted at her,
And such a noble carriage. How now Sirrah?

[Enter a **BOY**.

BOY
Sir, the great English Lady.

MIRABELL
What of her, Sir?

BOY
Has newly left her coach, and coming this way,
Where you may see her plain: Monsieur Pinac,
The only man that leads her.

[Enter **PINAC**, **MARIANA** and **ATTENDANTS**.

MIRABELL
He is much honored;
Would I had such a favour: now vex Ladies,
Envy, and vex, and rail.

ROSALURA
Ye are short of us, Sir.

MIRABELL
'Bless your fair fortune, Sir.

PINAC
I nobly thank ye.

MIRABELL
Is she married, friend?

PINAC
No, no.

MIRABELL
A goodly Lady;
A sweet and delicate aspect: mark, mark, and wonder!
Hast thou any hope of her?

PINAC
A little.

MIRABELL
Follow close then:
Lose not that hope.

PINAC
To you, Sir.

MIRABELL
Gentle Lady.

ROSALURA
She is fair indeed.

LILLIA-BIANCA
I have seen a fairer, yet
She is well.

ROSALURA
Her clothes sit handsom too.

LILLIA-BIANCA
She dresses prettily.

ROSALURA
And by my faith she is rich, she looks still sweeter.

A well bred woman, I warrant her.

LILLIA-BIANCA
Do you hear, Sir;
May I crave this Gentlewomans name?

PINAC
Mariana, Lady.

LILLIA-BIANCA
I will not say I ow ye a quarel Monsieur
For making me your Stale: a noble Gentleman
Would have had more courtesie; at least, more faith,
Than to turn off his Mistris at first trial:
You know not what respect I might have shew'd ye;
I find ye have worth.

PINAC
I cannot stay to answer ye;
Ye see my charge: I am beholding to ye
For all your merry tricks ye put upon me,
Your bobs, and base accounts: I came to love ye,
To wooe ye, and to serve ye; I am much indebted to ye
For dancing me off my legs; and then for walking me;
For telling me strange tales I never heard of,
More to abuse me; for mistaking me,
When ye both knew I was a Gentleman,
And one deserv'd as rich a match as you are.

LILLIA-BIANCA
Be not so bitter, Sir.

PINAC
You see this Lady:
She is young enough, and fair enough to please me,
A woman of a loving mind, a quiet,
And one that weighs the worth of him that loves her,
I am content with this, and bless my fortune,
Your curious Wits, and Beauties.

LILLIA-BIANCA
Faith see me once more.

PINAC
I dare not trouble ye.

LILLIA-BIANCA
May I speak to your Lady?

PINAC

I pray ye content your self: I know ye are bitter,
And in your bitterness, ye may abuse her;
Which if she comes to know, (for she understands ye not)
It may breed such a quarrel to your kindred,
And such an indiscretion fling on you too;
For she is nobly friended.

LILLIA-BIANCA

I could eat her.

PINAC

Rest as ye are, a modest noble Gentlewoman,
And afford your honest neighbours some of your prayers.

[Exit.

MIRABELL

What think you now?

LILLIA-BIANCA

Faith she's a pretty Whiting;
She has got a pretty catch too.

MIRABELL

You are angry;
Monstrous angry now; grievously angry;
And the pretty heart does swell now.

LILLIA-BIANCA

No in troth, Sir.

MIRABELL

And it will cry anon; a pox upon it:
And it will curse it self: and eat no meat, Lady;
And it will fight.

LILLIA-BIANCA

Indeed you are mistaken;
It will be very merry.

ROSALURA

Why, Sir, do you think
There are no more men living, nor no handsomer
Than he, or you, By this light there be ten thousand?
Ten thousand thousand: comfort your self, dear Monsieur,
Faces, and bodies, Wits, and all Abiliments

There are so many we regard 'em not.

[Enter **BELLEUR** and two **GENTLEMEN**.

MIRABELL
That such a noble Lady, I could burst now,
So far above such trifles?

BELLEUR
You did laugh at me,
And I know why ye laughed.

1ST GENTLEMAN
I pray ye be satisfied;
If we did laugh, we had some private reason,
And not at you.

2ND GENTLEMAN
Alas, we know you not, Sir.

BELLEUR
I'le make you know me; set your faces soberly;
Stand this way, and look sad; I'le be no May-game;
Sadder; demurer yet.

ROSALURA
What's the matter?
What ails this Gentleman?

BELLEUR
Go off now backward, that I may behold ye;
And not a simper on your lives.

LILLIA-BIANCA
He's mad sure.

BELLEUR
Do you observe me too?

MIRABELL
I may look on ye.

BELLEUR
Why do you grin? I know your minde.

MIRABELL
You do not,
You are strangely humorous: is there no mirth, nor pleasure,

But you must be the object?

BELLEUR
Mark, and observe me;
Where ever I am nam'd;
The very word shall raise a general sadness,
For the disgrace this scurvy woman did me;
This proud pert thing; take heed ye laugh not at me;
Provoke me not, take heed.

ROSALURA
I would fain please ye;
Do any thing to keep ye quiet.

BELLEUR
Hear me,
Till I receive a satisfaction
Equal to the disgrace, and scorn ye gave me:
Ye are a wretched woman; till thou woo'st me,
And I scorn thee asmuch, as seriously
Jear, and abuse thee; ask what Gill thou art;
Or any baser name; I will proclaim thee;
I will so sing thy vertue; so be-paint thee.

ROSALURA
Nay, good Sir, be more modest.

BELLEUR
Do you laugh again?
Because ye are a woman ye are lawless,
And out of compass of an honest anger.

ROSALURA
Good Sir, have a better belief of me.

LILLIA-BIANCA
Away dear Sister.

[Exit.

MIRABELL
Is not this better now, this seeming madness,
Than falling out with your friends?

BELLEUR
Have I not frighted her?

MIRABELL

Into her right wits, I warrant thee: follow this humor,
And thou shalt see how prosperously 'twill guide thee.

BELLEUR
I am glad I have found a way to woo yet, I was afraid once
I never should have made a civil Suiter.
Well, I'le about it still.

[Exit.

MIRABELL
Do, do, and prosper.
What sport do I make with these fools! What pleasure
Feeds me, and fats my sides at their poor innocence!

[Enter Leverduce, alias **LUGIER**, **Mr. ILLIARD.**

Wooing and wiving, hang it: give me mirth,
Witty and dainty mirth: I shall grow in love sure
With mine own happy head. Who's this? To me, Sir?
What youth is this?

LUGIER
Yes, Sir, I would speak with you,
If your name be Monsieur Mirabel.

MIRABELL
Ye have hit it,
Your business, I beseech ye?

LUGIER
This it is, Sir,
There is a Gentlewoman hath long time affected ye,
And lov'd ye dearly.

MIRABELL
Turn over, and end that story,
'Tis long enough: I have no faith in women, Sir.

LUGIER
It seems so, Sir: I do not come to woo for her,
Or sing her praises, though she well deserve 'em,
I come to tell ye, ye have been cruel to her,
Unkind and cruel, falser of faith, and careless,
Taking more pleasure in abusing her,
Wresting her honour to your wild disposes,
Than noble in requiting her affection:
Which, as ye are a man, I must desire ye

(A Gentleman of rank) not to persist in,
No more to load her fair name with your injuries.

MIRABELL
Why, I beseech ye, Sir?

LUGIER
Good Sir, I'le tell ye,
And I'le be short: I'le tell ye, because I love ye,
Because I would have you shun the shame may follow:
There is a noble man, new come to Town, Sir,
A noble and a great man that affects her,
A Countrey-man of mine, a brave Savoyan,
Nephew to th'Duke, and so much honours her,
That 'twill be dangerous to pursue your old way,
To touch at any thing concerns her honour,
Believe, most dangerous: her name is Oriana,
And this great man will marry her: take heed, Sir;
For howsoe'r her Brother, a staid Gentleman,
Lets things pass upon better hopes, this Lord, Sir,
Is of that fiery, and that poynant metal,
(Especially provok'd on by affection)
That 'twill be hard: but you are wise.

MIRABELL
A Lord, Sir?

LUGIER
Yes, and a noble Lord.

MIRABELL
'Send her good fortune,
This will not stir her Lord; a Barronness,
Say ye so; say ye so? by'r Lady, a brave title;
Top, and top gallant now; 'save her great Ladiship.
I was a poor servant of hers, I must confess, Sir,
And in those daies, I thought I might be jovy,
And make a little bold to call into her:
But Basto, now; I know my rules and distance;
Yet, if she want an Usher; such an implement;
One that is throughly pac'd; a clean made Gentleman;
Can hold a hanging up; with approbation
Plant his hat formally, and wait with patience
I do beseech you, Sir.

LUGIER
Sir, leave your scoffing;
And as ye are a Gentleman, deal fairly:

I have given ye a friends counsel, so I'le leave ye.

MIRABELL
But hark ye, hark ye, Sir; is't possible
I may believe what you say?

LUGIER
You may chuse, Sir.

MIRABELL
No Baits? No Fish-hooks, Sir? No Gins? No Nooses?
No Pitfals to catch Puppies?

LUGIER
I tell ye certain;
You may believe; if not, stand to the danger.

[Exeunt.

MIRABELL
A Lord of Savoy saies he? The Dukes Nephew?
A man so mighty? By 'Lady a fair marriage;
By my faith, a handsom fortune: I must leave prating;
For to confess the truth, I have abused her,
For which I should be sorry, but that will seem scurvy;
I must confess, she was ever since I knew her
As modest, as she was fair: I am sure she lov'd me;
Her means good; and her breeding excellent;
And for my sake she has refus'd fair matches:
I may play the fool finely. Stay who are these?

[Enter **De-GARD**, **ORIANA** and **ATTENDANTS**.

'Tis she, I am sure; and that the Lord it should seem,
He carries a fair Port; is a handsom man too:
I do begin to feel, I am a Coxcomb.

ORIANA
Good my Lord, chuse a nobler: for I know
I am so far below your rank and honour,
That what ye can say this way, I must credit
But spoken to beget your self sport: Alas, Sir,
I am so far off from deserving you,
My beauty so unfit for your Affection,
That I am grown the scorn of common Railers,
Of such injurious things, that when they cannot
Reach at my person, lie with my reputation:
I am poor besides.

De GARD
Ye are all wealth and goodness;
And none but such as are the scum of men,
The Ulcers of an honest state; Spight-weavers,
That live on poyson only, like swoln spiders,
Dare once profane such excellence, such sweetness.

MIRABELL
This man speaks loud indeed.

De GARD
Name but the men, Lady;
Let me but know these poor, and base depravers;
Lay but to my revenge their persons open,
And you shall see how suddenly, how fully
For your most beauteous sake, how direfully
I'le handle their despights. Is this thing one?
Be what he will.

MIRABELL
Sir.

De GARD
Dare your malicious tongue, Sir?

MIRABELL
I know you not; nor what you mean.

ORIANA
Good my Lord.

De GARD
If he, or any he.

ORIANA
I beseech your honour.
This Gentleman's a stranger to my knowledge,
And no doubt, Sir, a worthy man.

De GARD
Your mercy;
But had he been a tainter of your honour;
A blaster of those beauties raign within ye;
But we shall find a fitter time: dear Lady,
As soon as I have freed ye from your Guardian,
And done some honour'd offices unto ye,
I'le take ye with those faults the world flings on ye;

And dearer than the whole world I'le esteem ye.

[Exeunt.

MIRABELL
This is a thundring Lord; I am glad I scap'd him:
How lovingly the wench disclaim'd my villany!
I am vext now heartily that he shall have her;
Not that I care to marry, or to lose her;
But that this Bilbo-Lord shall reap that Maiden-head
That was my due; that he shall rig and top her;
I'de give a thousand Crowns now, he might miss her.

[Enter a **SERVANT**.

SERVANT
Nay, if I bear your blows, and keep your counsel,
You have good luck, Sir; I'le teach ye to strike lighter.

MIRABELL
Come hither, honest fellow; canst thou tell me
Where this great Lord lies? This Savoy Lord? Thou met'st him;
He now went by thee certain.

SERVANT
Yes, he did, Sir;
I know him; and I know you are fool'd.

MIRABELL
Come hither,
Here's all this, give me truth.

SERVANT
Not for your mony;
(And yet that may do much) but I have been beaten:
And by the worshipfull Contrivers beaten, and I'le tell ye;
This is no Lord, no Savoy Lord.

MIRABELL
Go forward.

SERVANT
This is a Trick, and put upon ye grosly
By one Lugier; the Lord is Monsieur de-Gard, Sir;
An honest Gentleman, and a neighbour here;
Their ends you understand better than I, sure.

MIRABELL

Now I know him.
Know him now plain.

SERVANT
I have discharg'd my colours; so God b'y ye, sir.

[Exit.

MIRABELL
What a purblinde Puppy was I; now I remember him.
All the whole cast on's face, though 'twere umber'd,
And mask'd with patches: what a dunder-whelp
To let him domineer thus: how he strutted,
And what a load of Lord he clapt upon him!
Would I had him here again, I would so bounce him,
I would so thank his Lordship for his lewd plot:
Do they think to carry it away, with a great band made of bird-pots,
And a pair of pin-buttockt breeches? Ha! 'Tis he again.
He comes, he comes, he comes; have at him.

[Enter **De-GARD**, **ORIANA**, &c.

[Sings.

My Savoy Lord, why dost thou frown on me?
And will that favour never sweeter be?
Wilt thou I say, for ever play the fool?
De-Gard be wise, and Savoy go to School.
My Lord De-Gard, I thank ye for your Antick;
My Lady bright, that will be sometimes Frantick;
You worthy Train, that wait upon this Pair,
'Send you more wit, and they a bouncing Baire
And so I take my humble leave of your honours.

[Exit.

De GARD
We are discover'd, there's no remedy
Lilia Biancha's man upon my life,
In stubbornness, because Lugier corrected him.
(A shameless slaves plague on him for a Rascal.)

ORIANA
I was in a perfect hope; the bane on't is now,
He will make mirth on mirth, to persecute us.

De GARD
We must be patient; I am vext to the proof too,

I'le try once more; then if I fail: Here's one speaks.

ORIANA
Let me be lost, and scorn'd first.

De GARD
Well, we'll consider,
Away, and let me shift; I shall be hooted else.

[Exeunt.

Enter **LUGIER, LILLIA-BIANCA, SERVANTS.**

LUGIER
Faint not; but do as I direct ye, trust me;
Believe me too, for what I have told ye, Lady,
As true as you are Lilia, is Authentick;
I know it; I have found it; 'tis a poor courage
Flies off for one repulse; these Travellers
Shall find before we have done, a home-spun wit,
A plain French understanding may cope with 'em;
They have had the better yet, thank your sweet Squire, here;
And let 'em brag: you would be reveng'd?

LILLIA-BIANCA
Yes surely.

LUGIER
And married too?

LILLIA-BIANCA
I think so.

LUGIER
Then be Counsel'd,
You know how to proceed: I have other Irons
Heating as well as yours: and I will strike
Three blows with one Stone home, be rul'd, and happie;
And so I leave ye. Now is the time.

LILLIA-BIANCA
I am ready,

If he do come to do me.

SERVANT
Will ye stand here,
And let the people think, ye are God knows what Mistris?
Let Boys, and Prentices presume upon ye?

LILLIA-BIANCA
Pre'thee hold thy peace.

SERVANT
Stand at his dore, that hates ye?

LILLIA-BIANCA
Pre'thee leave prating.

SERVANT
'Pray ye go to th' Tavern. I'le give ye a Pint of wine there,
If any of the Mad-cap Gentlemen should come by
That take up women upon speciall warrant,
You were in a wise case now.

[Enter **MIRABELL, PINAC, MARIANA, PRIEST, ATTENDANTS.**

LILLIA-BIANCA
Give me the Garland,
And wait you here.

MIRABELL
She is here to seek thee, Sirrah.
I told thee what would follow; she is mad for thee;
Shew, and advance. So early stirring Lady?
It shews a busie mind, a fancie troubled:
A willow Garland too? Is't possible?
'Tis pity so much beautie should lie mustie,
But 'tis not to be help'd now.

LILLIA-BIANCA
The more's my Miserie.
Good fortune to ye, Ladie, you deserve it:
To me, too late Repentance; I have sought it:
I do not envy, though I grieve a little,
You are Mistris of that happiness, those Joyes
That might have been, had I been wise: but fortune.

PINAC
She understands ye not, 'pray ye do not trouble her;
And do not cross me like a Hare thus, 'tis as ominous.

LILLIA-BIANCA

I come not to upbraid your Levitie
Though ye made shew of Love, and though I lik'd ye
To claim an interest; we are yet both Strangers,
But what we might have been, had you persever'd, Sir,
To be an eye-sore to your loving Lady;
This garland shews, I give my self forsaken;
(Yet she must pardon me, 'tis most unwillingly:)
And all the power and interest I had in ye;
As I perswade my self, somewhat ye lov'd me;
Thus patiently I render up, I offer
To her that must enjoy ye: and so bless ye;
Only, I heartily desire this Courtesie,
And would not be deni'd: to wait upon ye
This day, to see ye ty'd, then no more trouble ye.

PINAC

It needs not, Ladie.

LILLIA-BIANCA

Good Sir, grant me so much.

PINAC

'Tis private, and we make no invitation.

LILLIA-BIANCA

My presence, Sir, shall not proclaim it publick.

PINAC

May be 'tis not in Town.

LILLIA-BIANCA

I have a Coach, Sir,
And a most ready will to do you service.

MIRABELL

Strike now or never; make it sure: I tell thee,
She will hang her self, if she have thee not.

PINAC

'Pray ye, Sir,
Entertain my noble Mistris: only a word or two
With this importunate woman, and I'le relieve ye.
Now ye see what your flings are, and your fancies,
Your states, and your wild stubborness, now ye find
What 'tis to gird and kick at mens fair services,
To raise your pride to such a pitch, and glory

That goodness shews like gnats, scorn'd under ye,
'Tis ugly, naught, a self will in a woman,
Chain'd to an over-weening thought, is pestilent,
Murthers fair fortune first; then fair opinion:
There stands a Pattern, a true patient Pattern,
Humble, and sweet.

LILLIA-BIANCA

I can but grieve my ignorance,
Repentance some say too, is the best sacrifice;
For sure, Sir, if my chance had been so happy,
(As I confess I was mine own destroyer)
As to have arrived at you; I will not prophesie,
But certain, as I think, I should have pleas'd ye;
Have made ye as much wonder at my courtesie,
My love, and duty, as I have dishearten'd ye,
Some hours we have of youth, and some of folly;
And being free-born Maids, we take a liberty,
And to maintain that, sometimes we strain highly.

PINAC

Now ye talk reason.

LILLIA-BIANCA

But being yoak'd, and govern'd,
Married, and those light vanities purg'd from us;
How fair we grow, how gentle, and how tender,
We twine about those loves that shoot-up with us!
A sullen woman fear, that talks not to ye;
She has a sad and darkn'd soul, loves dully:
A merry and a free wench, give her liberty;
Believe her in the lightest form she appears to ye,
Believe her excellent, though she despise ye,
Let but these fits and flashes pass, she will shew to ye;
As Jewels rub'd from dust, or Gold new burnish'd:
Such had I been, had you believ'd.

PINAC

Is't possible?

LILLIA-BIANCA

And to your happiness, I dare assure ye
If True love be accounted so; your pleasure,
Your will, and your command had tyed my Motions:
But that hope's gone; I know you are young, and giddy,
And till you have a Wife can govern with ye,
You sail upon this world-Sea, light and empty;
Your Bark in danger daily; 'tis not the name neither

Of Wife can steer ye; but the noble nature,
The diligence, the care, the love, the patience,
She makes the Pilot, and preserves the Husband,
That knows, and reckons every Rib he is built on;
But this I tell ye, to my shame.

PINAC

I admire ye,
And now am sorry, that I aim beyond ye.

MIRABELL

So, so, so, fair and softly. She is thine own, Boy,
She comes now, without Lure.

PINAC

But that it must needs
Be reckon'd to me as a wantonness,
Or worse, a madness, to forsake a Blessing,
A Blessing of that hope.

LILLIA-BIANCA

I dare not urge ye,
And yet, dear Sir.

PINAC

'Tis most certain, I had rather,
If 'twere in my own choice, for you are my country-woman,
A Neighbour, here born by me, she a Stranger;
And who knows how her friends?

LILLIA-BIANCA

Do as you please, Sir,
If ye be fast; not all the World; I love ye,
'Tis most true, and clear, I would perswade ye;
And I shall love you still.

PINAC

Go, get before me;
So much you have won upon me; do it presently:
Here's a Priest ready; I'll have you.

LILLIA-BIANCA

Not now, Sir,
No, you shall pardon me; advance your Lady,
I dare not hinder your most high Preferment,
'Tis honour enough for me I have unmask'd ye.

PINAC

How's that?

LILLIA-BIANCA
I have caught ye, Sir, alas, I am no States-woman,
Nor no great Traveller, yet I have found ye,
I have found your Lady too, your beauteous Lady;
I have found her birth and breeding too, her discipline;
Who brought her over, and who kept your Lady;
And when he laid her by, what vertuous Nunnery
Receiv'd her in; I have found all these: are ye blank now?
Methinks such travel'd wisdoms should not fool thus;
Such excellent indiscretions.

MIRABELL
How could she know this?

LILLIA-BIANCA
'Tis true, she's English born, but most part French now,
And so I hope you'll find her, to your comfort,
Alas, I am ignorant of what she cost ye;
The price of these hired cloaths I do not know Gentlemen;
Those Jewels are the Brokers, how ye stand bound for 'em.

PINAC
Will you make this good?

LILLIA-BIANCA
Yes, yes, and to her face, Sir,
That she is an English Whore, a kind of fling dust,
One of your London Light o' Loves; a right one,
Came over in thin Pumps, and half a Petticoat,
One Faith, and one Smock, with a broken Haberdasher;
I know all this without a Conjurer;
Her name is jumping-Joan, an ancient Sin-Weaver;
She was first a Ladies Chamber-maid, there slip'd
And broke her leg above the knee; departed
And set up shop her self. Stood the fierce Conflicts
Of many a furious Term; there lost her colours,
And last ship'd over hither.

MIRABELL
We are betray'd.

LILLIA-BIANCA
Do you come to fright me with this mystery?
To stir me with a stink none can endure, Sir?
I pray ye proceed, the Wedding will become ye;
Who gives the Lady? you? an excellent Father;

A careful man, and one that knows a Beauty,
'Send ye fair Shipping, Sir, and so I'll leave ye,
Be wise and manly, then I may chance to love ye.

[Exit.

MIRABELL
As I live I am asham'd, this wench has reach'd me,
Monstrous asham'd, but there's no remedy,
This skew'd eye'd Carrion.

PINAC
This I suspected ever,
Come, come, uncase, we have no more use of ye;
Your Cloaths must back again.

MARIANA
Sir, ye shall pardon me;
'Tis not our English use to be degraded;
If you will visit me, and take your venture,
You shall have pleasure for your properties;
And so sweet heart.

MIRABELL
Let her go, and the Devil go with her;
We have never better luck with these preludiums;
Come, be not daunted; think she is but a woman,
And let her have the Devils wit, we'll reach her.

[Exeunt.

SCÆNA SECUNDA

Enter **ROSALURA** and **LUGIER**.

ROSALURA
Ye have now redeem'd my good opinion, Tutor,
And ye stand fair again.

LUGIER
I can but labour,
And sweat in your affairs; I am sure Belleur
Will be here instantly, and use his anger,
His wonted harshness.

ROSALURA

I hope he will not beat me.

LUGIER
No sure, he has more manners; be you ready.

ROSALURA
Yes, yes, I am, and am resolv'd to fit him,
With patience to outdo all he can offer;
But how does Oriana?

LUGIER
Worse, and worse still;
There is a sad house for her: she is now,
Poor Lady, utterly distracted.

ROSALURA
Pity!
Infinite pity! 'tis a handsome Lady,
That Mirabel's a Beast, worse than a Monster,
If this affliction work not.

[Enter **LILLIA-BIANCA**.

LILLIA-BIANCA
Are ye ready?
Belleur is coming on, here, hard behind me,
I have no leisure to relate my Fortune.
Only I wish you may come off as handsomely,
Upon the sign you know what.

[Exit.

ROSALURA
Well, well, leave me.

[Enter **BELLEUR**.

BELLEUR
How now?

ROSALURA
Ye are welcome, Sir.

BELLEUR
'Tis well ye have manners:
That Court'sie again, and hold your Countenance stai'dly;
That look's too light; take heed: so, sit ye down now,
And to confirm me that your Gall is gone,

Your bitterness dispers'd, for so I'll have it:
Look on me stedfastly, and whatsoe'r I say unto ye,
Move not, nor alter in your face, ye are gone then:
For if you do express the least distaste,
Or shew an angry wrinkle, mark me, woman,
We are now alone, I will so conjure thee;
The third part of my Execution
Cannot be spoke.

ROSALURA

I am at your dispose, Sir.

BELLEUR

Now rise, and woo me a little, let me hear that faculty:
But touch me not, nor do not lie I charge ye.
Begin now.

ROSALURA

If so mean and poor a Beauty
May ever hope the Grace.

BELLEUR

Ye cog, ye flatter,
Like a lewd thing ye lie: may hope that grace?
Why, what grace canst thou hope for? Answer not,
For if thou dost, and liest again I'll swindge thee:
Do not I know thee for a pestilent Woman?
A proud at both ends? Be not angry,
Nor stir not o' your life.

ROSALURA

I am counsell'd, Sir.

BELLEUR

Art thou not now (confess, for I'll have the truth out)
As much unworthy of a man of merit,
Or any of ye all? Nay, of meer man?
Though he were crooked, cold, all wants upon him:
Nay, of any dishonest thing that bears that figure:
As Devils are of mercy?

ROSALURA

We are unworthy.

BELLEUR

Stick to that truth, and it may chance to save thee.
And is it not our bounty that we take ye?
That we are troubled, vex'd, or tortur'd with ye?

Our meer and special bounty?

ROSALURA
Yes.

BELLEUR
Our pity,
That for your wickedness we swindge ye soundly;
Your stubbornness, and your stout hearts, we be-labour ye,
Answer to that.

ROSALURA
I do confess your pity.

BELLEUR
And dost not thou deserve in thine own person?
(Thou Impudent, thou Pert; do not change countenance.)

ROSALURA
I dare not, Sir.

BELLEUR
For if ye do.

ROSALURA
I am setled.

BELLEUR
Thou Wag-tail, Peacock, Puppy, look on me:
I am a Gentleman.

ROSALURA
It seems no less, Sir.

BELLEUR
And darest thou in thy Surquedry?

ROSALURA
I beseech ye;
It was my weakness, Sir, I did not view ye,
I took no notice of your noble parts,
Nor call'd your person, nor your proper fashion.

BELLEUR
This is some amends yet.

ROSALURA
I shall mend, Sir, daily,

And study to deserve.

BELLEUR
Come a little nearer;
Canst thou repent thy villainy?

ROSALURA
Most seriously.

BELLEUR
And be asham'd?

ROSALURA
I am asham'd.

BELLEUR
Cry.

ROSALURA
It will be hard to do, Sir.

BELLEUR
Cry instantly;
Cry monstrously, that all the Town may hear thee;
Cry seriously, as if thou hadst lost thy Monkey;
And as I like thy tears.

[Enter **LILLIA-BIANCA**, and four **WOMEN** laughing.

ROSALURA
Now.

BELLEUR
How? how? do ye jear me?
Have ye broke your bounds again, Dame?

ROSALURA
Yes, and laugh at ye,
And laugh most heartily.

BELLEUR
What are these, Whirl-winds?
Is Hell broke loose, and all the Furies flutter'd?
Am I greas'd once again?

ROSALURA
Yes indeed are ye;
And once again ye shall be, if ye quarrel;

Do you come to vent your fury on a Virgin?
Is this your Manhood, Sir?

1ST WOMAN
Let him do his best,
Let's see the utmost of his indignation,
I long to see him angry; Come, proceed, Sir.
Hang him, he dares not stir, a man of Timber.

2ND WOMAN
Come hither to fright maids with thy Bul-faces?
To threaten Gentlewomen? Thou a man? A May-pole,
A great dry Pudding.

3RD WOMAN
Come, come, do your worst, Sir;
Be angry if thou darst.

BELLEUR
The Lord deliver me!

4TH WOMAN
Do but look scurvily upon this Lady,
Or give us one foul word. We are all mistaken,
This is some mighty Dairy-maid in Mans Cloaths.

LILLIA-BIANCA
I am of that mind too.

BELLEUR
What will they do to me!

LILLIA-BIANCA
And hired to come and abuse us; a man has manners;
A Gentleman, Civility, and Breeding:
Some Tinkers Trull, with a Beard glew'd on.

1ST WOMAN
Let's search him;
And as we find him.

BELLEUR
Let me but depart from ye,
Sweet Christian-women.

LILLIA-BIANCA
Hear the Thing speak, Neighbours.

BELLEUR

'Tis but a small request; if e'r I trouble ye,
If e'r I talk again of beating Women,
Or beating any thing that can but turn to me;
Of ever thinking of a handsome Lady
But vertuously and well; of ever speaking
But to her honour; This I'll promise ye,
I will take Rhubarb, and purge Choler mainly,
Abundantly I'll purge.

LILLIA-BIANCA

I'll send ye Broths, Sir.

BELLEUR

I will be laugh'd at, and endure it patiently,
I will do any thing.

ROSALURA

I'll be your Bayl then;
When ye come next to woo, 'pray come not boisterously,
And furnish'd like a Bear-ward.

BELLEUR

No in truth, forsooth.

ROSALURA

I scented ye long since.

BELLEUR

I was to blame sure,
I will appear a Gentleman.

ROSALURA

'Tis the best for ye,
For a true noble Gentleman's a brave thing;
Upon that hope we quit ye. You fear seriously?

BELLEUR

Yes truly do I; I confess I fear ye,
And honour ye, and any thing.

ROSALURA

Farewel then.

WOMEN

And when ye come to woo next bring more mercy.

[Exeunt.

[Enter two **GENTLEMEN**.

BELLEUR
A Dairy-maid! a Tinkers-Trull! Heaven bless me!
Sure if I had provok'd 'em, they had quarter'd me.
I am a most ridiculous Ass, now I perceive it:
A Coward, and a Knave too.

1ST GENTLEMAN
'Tis the mad Gentleman:
Let's set our Faces right.

BELLEUR
No, no, laugh at me;
And laugh aloud.

2ND GENTLEMAN
We are better manner'd, Sir.

BELLEUR
I do deserve it; call me Patch, and Puppy,
And beat me if you please.

1ST GENTLEMAN
No indeed, we know ye.

BELLEUR
'Death, do as I would have ye.

2ND GENTLEMAN
You are an Ass then;
A Coxcomb, and a Calf.

BELLEUR
I am a great Calf;
Kick me a little now: Why, when? Sufficient:
Now laugh aloud, and scorn me; so good b'ye;
And ever when ye meet me laugh.

1ST GENTLEMAN
We will, Sir.

[Exeunt.

SCÆNA TERTIA

Enter **NANTOLET**, **LA-CASTRE**, **De-GARD**, **LUGIER**, **MIRABELL**.

MIRABELL
Your patience, Gentlemen: why do ye bait me?

NANTOLET
Is't not a shame you are so stubborn hearted,
So stony and so dull to such a Lady,
Of her Perfections, and her Misery?

LUGIER
Does she not love ye? does not her distraction
For your sake only, her most pitied lunacie
Of all but you, shew ye? does it not compel ye?

MIRABELL
Soft and fair, Gentlemen, pray ye proceed temperately.

LUGIER
If ye have any feeling, any sense in ye,
The least touch of a noble heart.

LA-CASTRE
Let him alone;
It is his glory that he can kill Beauty,
Ye bear my Stamp, but not my Tenderness;
Your wild unsavoury Courses set that in ye!
For shame, be sorry, though ye cannot cure her,
Shew something of a Man, of a fair Nature.

MIRABELL
Ye make me mad.

De-GARD
Let me pronounce this to ye,
You take a strange felicity in slighting
And wronging Women, which my poor Sister feels now,
Heavens hand be gentle on her: Mark me, Sir,
That very hour she dies, there's small hope otherwise,
That minute you and I must grapple for it,
Either your life or mine.

MIRABELL
Be not so hot, Sir,
I am not to be wrought on by these policies,
In truth I am not; Nor do I fear the tricks,
Or the high sounding threats of a Savoyan;

I glory not in Cruelty, ye wrong me;
Nor grow up water'd with the tears of Women;
This let me tell ye, howsoe'r I shew to ye,
Wild, as ye please to call it, or self-will'd;
When I see cause I can both do and suffer,
Freely, and feelingly, as a true Gentleman.

[Enter **ROSALURA** and **LILLIA-BIANCA**.

ROSALURA
O pity, pity, thousand, thousand pities!

LILLIA-BIANCA
Alas poor Soul! she will dye; she is grown sensless;
She will not know, nor speak now.

ROSALURA
Dye for love!
And love of such a Youth! I would dye for a Dog first,
He that kills me I'll give him leave to eat me;
I'll know men better ere I sigh for any of 'em.

LILLIA-BIANCA
Ye have done a worthy act, Sir; a most famous;
Ye have kill'd a Maid the wrong way, ye are a conqueror.

ROSALURA
A Conquerour? a Cobler; hang him Sowter;
Go hide thy self for shame, go lose thy memory;
Live not 'mongst Men; thou art a Beast, a Monster;
A Blatant Beast.

LILLIA-BIANCA
If ye have yet any honesty,
Or ever heard of any; take my Counsel;
Off with your Garters: and seek out a Bough,
A handsom Bough; (for I would have ye hang like a Gentleman;)
And write some doleful matter to the World,
A Warning to hard hearted men.

MIRABELL
Out Kitlings:
What Catterwauling's here? what Gibbing?
Do you think my heart is softned with a black Santis?
Shew me some reason.

[Enter **ORIANA** on a Bed.

ROSALURA
Here then, here is a reason.

NANTOLET
Now, if ye be a man, let this sight shake ye.

La-CASTRE
Alas poor Gentlewoman! do you know me, Lady?

LUGIER
How she looks up, and stares!

ORIANA
I know ye very well;
You are my Godfather; and that's the Monsieur.

De GARD
And who am I?

ORIANA
You are Amadis de Gaul, Sir.
Oh oh, my heart! were ye never in love, sweet Lady?
And do you never dream of Flowers and Gardens?
I dream of walking Fires; take heed, it comes now;
Who's that? pray stand away; I have seen that face sure;
How light my head is!

ROSALURA
Take some rest.

ORIANA
I cannot,
For I must be up to morrow to go to Church,
And I must dress me, put my new Gown on,
And be as fine to meet my Love: Heigh ho!
Will not you tell me where my Love lies buried?

MIRABELL
He is not dead: beshrew my heart, she stirs me.

ORIANA
He is dead to me.

MIRABELL
Is't possible my Nature
Should be so damnable, to let her suffer?
Give me your hand.

ORIANA
How soft you feel, how gentle!
I'll tell you your fortune, Friend.

MIRABELL
How she stares on me!

ORIANA
You have a flattering face, but 'tis a fine one;
I warrant you may have a hundred Sweet-hearts;
Will ye pray for me? I shall dye to morrow,
And will ye ring the Bells?

MIRABELL
I am most unworthy,
I do confess, unhappy; do you know me?

ORIANA
I would I did.

MIRABELL
Oh fair tears, how ye take me!

ORIANA
Do you weep too? you have not lost your Lover;
You mock me; I'l go home, and pray.

MIRABELL
'Pray ye pardon me:
Or if it please ye to consider justly,
Scorn me, for I deserve it: Scorn, and shame me:
Sweet Oriana.

LILLIA-BIANCA
Let her alone, she trembles;
Her fits will grow more strong if ye provoke her.

La-CASTRE
Certain she knows ye not, yet loves to see ye:
How she smiles now!

[Enter **BELLEUR**.

BELLEUR
Where are ye? Oh, why do not you laugh? come, laugh at me;
What a Devil! art thou sad, and such a subject,
Such a ridiculous subject as I am
Before thy face?

MIRABELL

Prithee put off this lightness;
This is no time for mirth, nor place; I have us'd too much on't:
I have undone my self, and a sweet Lady,
By being too indulgent to my foolery,
Which truly I repent; look here.

BELLEUR

What ails she?

MIRABELL

Alas, she's mad.

BELLEUR

Mad?

MIRABELL

Yes, too sure for me too.

BELLEUR

Dost thou wonder at that? by this good light they are all so;
They are coz'ning mad, they are brawling mad, they are proud mad:
They are all, all mad; I came from a World of mad Women.
Mad as March-Hares; get 'em in Chains, then deal with 'em.
There's one that's mad; she seems well, but she is dog-mad.
Is she dead dost' think?

MIRABELL

Dead! Heaven forbid.

BELLEUR

Heaven further it;
For till they be key cold dead, there's no trusting of 'em,
Whate'r they seem, or howsoe'r they carry it,
Till they be chap-faln, and their Tongues at peace,
Nail'd in their Coffins sure, I'll ne'r believe 'em,
Shall I talk with her?

MIRABELL

No, dear friend, be quiet,
And be at peace a while.

BELLEUR

I'll walk aside,
And come again anon: but take heed to her,
You say she is a Woman?

MIRABELL
Yes.

BELLEUR
Take great heed:
For if she do not cozen thee, then hang me.
Let her be mad, or what she will, she'll cheat thee.

[Exit.

MIRABELL
Away, wild Fool: how vile this shews in him now!
Now take my faith, before ye all I speak it,
And with it, my repentant love.

La-CASTRE
This seems well.

MIRABELL
Were but this Lady clear again, whose sorrows
My very heart melts for; were she but perfect
(For thus to marry her would be two miseries,)
Before the richest and the noblest Beauty,
France, or the World could shew me; I would take her
As she is now, my Tears and Prayers shall wed her.

De GARD
This makes some small amends.

ROSALURA
She beckons to ye,
To us too, to go off.

NANTOLET
Let's draw aside all.

ORIANA
Oh my best friend; I would fain.

MIRABELL
What? she speaks well,
And with another voice.

ORIANA
But I am fearful,
And shame a little stops my tongue.

MIRABELL

Speak boldly.

ORIANA

Tell ye, I am well, I am perfect well: 'pray ye mock not;
And that I did this to provoke your Nature,
Out of my infinite and restless love,
To win your pity; pardon me.

MIRABELL

Go forward;
Who set ye on?

ORIANA

None, as I live, no Creature;
Not any knew, or ever dream'd what I meant;
Will ye be mine?

MIRABELL

'Tis true, I pity ye:
But when I marry ye, ye must be wiser:
Nothing but Tricks? Devices?

ORIANA

Will ye shame me?

MIRABELL

Yes, marry will I: Come near, come near, a miracle;
The Woman's well; she was only mad for Marriage,
Stark mad to be ston'd to death; give her good counsel,
Will this world never mend? are ye caught, Damsel?

[Enter **BELLEUR**, **LA-CASTRE**, **LUGIER**, **NANTOLET**, **De GARD**, **ROSALURA** and **BIANCA**.

BELLEUR

How goes it now?

MIRABELL

Thou art a kind of Prophet,
The Woman's well again, and would have gull'd me;
Well, excellent well: and not a taint upon her.

BELLEUR

Did not I tell ye? Let 'em be what can be;
Saints, Devils, any thing, they will abuse us;
Thou wert an Ass to believe her so long, a Coxcomb;
Give 'em a minute they'll abuse whole millions.

MIRABELL

And am not I a rare Physician, Gentlemen,
That can cure desperate mad minds?

De GARD
Be not insolent.

MIRABELL
Well, go thy waies: from this hour, I disclaim thee,
Unless thou hast a trick above this: then I'le love thee.
Ye owe me for your Cure; pray have a care of her,
For fear she fall into Relapse: come Belleur
We'll set up Bills, to Cure Diseased Virgins.

BELLEUR
Shall we be merry?

MIRABELL
Yes.

BELLEUR
But I'le no more projects;
If we could make 'em mad, it were some mastery.

[Exeunt.

LILLIA-BIANCA
I am glad she is well again.

ROSALURA
So am I, certain,
Be not ashamed.

ORIANA
I shall never see a man more.

De GARD
Come ye are a fool: had ye but told me this trick,
He should not have gloried thus.

LUGIER
He shall not long neither.

La-CASTRE
Be rul'd, and be at peace: ye have my consent,
And what power I can work with.

NANTOLET
Come, leave blushing;

We are your friends; an honest way compell'd ye;
Heaven will not see so true a love unrecompenc'd;
Come in, and slight him too.

LUGIER
The next shall hit him.

[Exeunt.

Enter **De GARD** and **LUGIER**.

De GARD
'T will be discover'd.

LUGIER
That's the worst can happen:
If there be any way to reach, and work upon him;
Upon his nature suddenly, and catch him: that he loves,
Though he dissemble it, and would shew contrary,
And will at length relent, I'le lay my Fortune,
Nay more, my life.

De GARD
Is she won?

LUGIER
Yes, and ready,
And my designments set.

De GARD
They are now for Travel,
All for that Game again: they have forgot wooing.

LUGIER
Let 'em; we'll travel with 'em.

De GARD
Where's his Father?

LUGIER
Within; he knows my mind too and allows it;
Pities your Sisters Fortune most sincerely;

And has appointed, for our more assistance,
Some of his secret Friends.

De GARD
'Speed the Plough.

LUGIER
Well said;
And be you serious too.

De GARD
I shall be diligent.

LUGIER
Let's break the Ice for one, the rest will drink too
(Believe me, Sir) of the same Cup; my young Gentlewomen
Wait but who sets the game a foot; though they seem stubborn,
Reserv'd, and proud now, yet I know their hearts,
Their Pulses how they beat, and for what cause, Sir;
And how they long to venture their Abilities
In a true Quarrel; Husbands they must, and will have,
Or Nunneries, and thin Collations
To cool their bloods; let's all about our business,
And if this fail, let Nature work.

De GARD
Ye have arm'd me.

[Exeunt.

SCÆNA SECUNDA

Enter **MIRABELL, NANTOLET** and **LA-CASTRE**.

La-CASTRE
Will ye be wilful then?

MIRABELL
'Pray, Sir, your pardon,
For I must Travel: lie lazy here,
Bound to a Wife? Chain'd to her subtleties,
Her humours, and her wills, which are meer Fetters;
To have her to day pleas'd, to morrow peevish,
The third day mad, the fourth rebellious?
You see, before they are married, what Moriscoes,
What Masques, and Mummeries they put upon us,

To be ty'd here, and suffer their Lavalto's?

NANTOLET
'Tis your own seeking.

MIRABELL
Yes, to get my freedom;
Were they as I could wish 'em.

La-CASTRE
Fools, and Meacocks,
To endure what you think fit to put upon 'em:
Come, change your mind.

MIRABELL
Not before I have chang'd Air, Father.
When I know Women worthy of my company,
I will return again and wait upon 'em;
Till then (dear Sir) I'le amble all the world over,
And run all hazards, misery, and poverty,

[Enter **PINAC** and **BELLEUR**.

So I escape the dangerous Bay of Matrimony.

PINAC
Are ye resolv'd?

MIRABELL
Yes certain; I will out again.

PINAC
We are for ye, Sir; we are your servants once more;
Once more we'll seek our fortune in strange Countries;
Ours is too scornful for us.

BELLEUR
Is there ne're a Land
That ye have read, or heard of, (for I care not how far it be,
Nor under what pestiferous Star it lies)
A happy Kingdom where there are no Women?
Nor have been ever? Nor no mention
Of any such lewd things, with lewder qualities?
For thither would I Travel; where 'tis Felony
To confess he had a Mother: a Mistris, Treason.

La-CASTRE
Are you for Travel too?

BELLEUR

For any thing;
For living in the Moon, and stopping hedges,
E're I stay here to be abus'd, and baffl'd.

NANTOLET

Why did ye not break your minds to me? they are my Daughters;
And sure I think I should have that command over 'em,
To see 'em well bestow'd: I know ye are Gentlemen,
Men of fair Parts and States; I know your Parents;
And had ye told me of your fair Affections—
Make but one tryal more; and let me second ye.

BELLEUR

No I'le make Hob-nails first, and mend old Kettles:
Can ye lend me an Armour of high proof, to appear in,
And two or three Field-pieces to defend me?
The Kings Guard are meer Pigmeys.

NANTOLET

They will not eat ye.

BELLEUR

Yes, and you too, and twenty fatter Monsieurs,
If their high stomachs hold: they came with Chopping-knives,
To cut me into Rands, and Sirloins, and so powder me.
Come, shall we go?

NANTOLET

You cannot be so discourteous
(If ye intend to go) as not to visit 'em,
And take your leaves.

MIRABELL

That we dare do, and civilly,
And thank 'em too.

PINAC

Yes, Sir, we know that honesty.

BELLEUR

I'le come i'th' Rear, forty foot off, I'le assure ye,
With a good Gun in my hand; I'le no more Amazons,
I mean, no more of their frights; I'le make my three legs
Kiss my hand twice; and if I smell no danger;
If the enterview be clear, may be I'le speak to her;
I'le wear a privy coat too; and behind me,

To make those parts secure, a Bandog.

LA-CASTRE
You are a merry Gentleman.

BELLEUR
A wary Gentleman; I do assure ye,
I have been warn'd, and must be arm'd.

LA-CASTRE
Well, Son,
These are your hasty thoughts, when I see you are bent to it,
Then I'le believe, and joyn with ye; So we'll leave ye:
There's a Trick will make ye stay.

NANTOLET
I hope so.

[Exeunt.

MIRABELL
We have won immortal Fame now, if we leave 'em.

PINAC
You have, but we have lost.

MIRABELL
Pinac, thou art cozen'd;
I know they love ye; and to gain ye handsomly,
Not to be thought to yield, they would give millions;
Their Fathers willingness, that must needs shew ye.

PINAC
If I thought so.

MIRABELL
Ye shall be hang'd, ye Recreant,
Would ye turn Renegado now?

BELLEUR
No let's away, Boys,
Out of the Air, and tumult of their Villanies;
Though I were married to that Grashopper,
And had her fast by th' legs I should think she would cozen me.

[Enter a young **FACTOR**.

FACTOR

Monsieur Mirabel, I take it?

MIRABELL
Y'are i'th' right, Sir.

FACTOR
I am come to seek ye, Sir; I have been at your Fathers,
And understanding you were here.

MIRABELL
Ye are welcom:
May I crave your name?

FACTOR
Foss, Sir, and your servant;
That you may know me better; I am Factor
To your old Merchant, Leverdure.

MIRABELL
How do's he?

FACTOR
Well, Sir, I hope: he is now at Orleance,
About some business.

MIRABELL
You are once more welcom,
Your Master's a right honest man; and one
I am much beholding to, and must very shortly
Trouble his love again.

FACTOR
You may be bold, Sir.

MIRABELL
Your business if you please now?

FACTOR
This it is, Sir,
I know ye well remember in your travel
A Genoa Merchant.

MIRABELL
I remember many.

FACTOR
But this man, Sir, particularly; your own benefit
Must needs imprint him in ye: one Alberto;

A Gentleman you sav'd from being Murther'd
A little from Bollonia,
I was then my self in Italie, and suppli'd ye,
Though haply, you have forgot me now.

MIRABELL
No, I remember ye,
And that Alberto too: a noble Gentleman:
More to remember, were to thank my self, Sir.
What of that Gentleman?

FACTOR
He is dead.

MIRABELL
I am sorry.

FACTOR
But on his death-bed, leaving to his Sister
All that he had, beside some certain Jewels,
Which with a Ceremony, he bequeath'd to you,
In gratefull memory: he commanded strictly
His Sister, as she lov'd him and his peace,
To see those Jewels safe, and true deliver'd;
And with them, his last love. She, as tender
To observe his will, not trusting friend, nor servant,
With such a weight, is come her self to Paris,
And at my Masters house.

MIRABELL
You tell me a wonder.

FACTOR
I tell ye a truth, Sir: She is young, and handsom,
And well attended: of much State, and Riches;
So loving, and obedient to her Brother;
That on my conscience, if he had given her also,
She would most willingly have made her tender.

MIRABELL
May not I see her?

FACTOR
She desires it heartily.

MIRABELL
And presently?

FACTOR
She is now about some business,
Passing accompts of some few debts here owing,
And buying Jewels of a Merchant.

MIRABELL
Is she wealthie?

FACTOR
I would ye had her, Sir, at all adventure,
Her Brother had a main State.

MIRABELL
And fair too?

FACTOR
The prime of all those parts of Italie,
For beautie, and for Courtesie.

MIRABELL
I must needs see her.

FACTOR
'Tis all her business, Sir. Ye may now see her,
But to morrow will be fitter for your visitation;
For she is not yet prepared.

MIRABELL
Only her sight, Sir;
And when you shall think fit for further visit.

FACTOR
Sir, ye may see her; and I'le wait your coming.

MIRABELL
And I'le be with ye instantly. I know the house,
Mean time, my love, and thanks, Sir.

FACTOR
Your poor Servant.

[Exit.

PINAC
Thou hast the strangest Luck: what was that Alberto?

MIRABELL
An honest noble Merchant, 'twas my chance

To rescue from some rogues had almost slain him;
And he in kindness to remember this.

BELLEUR
Now we shall have you,
For all your protestations, and your forwardness,
Find out strange fortunes in this Ladies eyes,
And new enticements to put off your journey;
And who shall have honour then?

MIRABELL
No, no, never fear it:
I must needs see her, to receive my Legacy.

BELLEUR
If it be ty'd up in her smock, heaven help thee:
May not we see too?

MIRABELL
Yes, afore we go:
I must be known my self e're I be able
To make thee welcom: wouldst thou see more women?
I thought you had been out of love with all.

BELLEUR
I may be,
I find that, with the least encouragement:
Yet I desire to see whether all Countries
Are naturally possess'd with the same spirits;
For if they be, I'le take a Monastery,
And never travel; for I had rather be a Frier,
And live mew'd up, than be a fool, and flouted.

MIRABELL
Well, well, I'le meet ye anon; then tell you more, boys;
How e'er stand prepar'd, prest for our journey;
For certain, we shall go, I think, when I have seen her,
And view'd her well.

PINAC
Go, go, and we'll wait for ye;
Your fortune directs ours.

BELLEUR
You shall find us i'th' Tavern,
Lamenting in Sack and Sugar for our losses;
If she be right Italian, and want servants,
You may prefer the properest man.

How I could worry a woman now!

PINAC
Come, come, leave prating;
Ye may have enough to do, without this boasting.

[Exeunt.

SCÆNA TERTIA

Enter **LUGIER**, **De-GARD**, **ROSALURA**, and **LILLIA-BIANCA**.

LUGIER
This is the last adventure.

De GARD
And the happiest,
As we hope too.

ROSALURA
We should be glad to find it.

LILLIA-BIANCA
Who shall conduct us thither?

LUGIER
Your man is ready,
For I must not be seen; no, nor this Gentleman;
That may beget suspicion: all the rest
Are people of no doubt; I would have ye, Ladies,
Keep your old liberties, and as we instruct ye:
Come, look not pale; you shall not lose your wishes;
Nor beg 'em neither: but be your selves, and happy.

ROSALURA
I tell ye true, I cannot hold off longer,
Nor give no more hard language.

De GARD
You shall not need.

ROSALURA
I love the Gentleman, and must now show it;
Shall I beat a proper man out of heart?

LUGIER

There's none advises ye.

LILLIA-BIANCA
'Faith I repent me too.

LUGIER
Repent, and spoil all,
Tell what ye know, ye had best.

LILLIA-BIANCA
I'le tell what I think;
For if he ask me now, if I can love him,
I'le tell him yes, I can: The man's a kind man;
And out of his true honesty affects me;
Although he plaid the fool, which I requited;
Must I still hold him at the staves end?

LUGIER
You are two strange women.

ROSALURA
We may be, if we fool still.

LUGIER
Dare ye believe me?
Follow but this advice I have set you in now,
And if ye lose: would ye yield now so basely?
Give up without your honours saved?

De GARD
Fie, Ladies.
Preserve your freedom still.

LILLIA-BIANCA
Well, well, for this time.

LUGIER
And carry that full state.

ROSALURA
That's as the wind stands:
If it begin to chop about, and scant us;
Hang me, but I know what I'le do: come direct us,
I make no doubt, we shall do handsomly.

De GARD
Some part o'th' way we'll wait upon ye, Ladies;
The rest your man supplies.

LUGIER
Do well, I'le honour ye.

[Exeunt.

Enter **FACTOR** and **MIRABELL**, **ORIANA** and two **MERCHANTS**.

FACTOR
Look ye, Sir, there she is, you see how busie;
Methinks you are infinitely bound to her, for her journey.

MIRABELL
How gloriously she shews! She is a tall woman.

FACTOR
Of a fair Size, Sir. My Master not being at home,
I have been so out of my wits, to get her company:
I mean, Sir, of her own fair sex, and fashion.

MIRABELL
Afar off, she is most fair too.

FACTOR
Near, most Excellent.
At length, I have entreated two fair Ladies,
And happily you know 'em: the young Daughters
Of Monsieur Nantolet.

MIRABELL
I know 'em well, Sir.
What are those? Jewels?

FACTOR
All.

MIRABELL
They make a rich shew!

FACTOR
There is a matter of ten thousand pounds too
Was owing here: you see those Merchants with her;
They have brought it in now.

MIRABELL

How handsomly her shape shews!

FACTOR

Those are still neat: your Italians are most curious:
Now she looks this way.

MIRABELL

She has a goodly presence,
How full of courtesie! Well, Sir, I'le leave ye,
And if I may be bold to bring a friend or two;
Good noble Gentlemen.

FACTOR

No doubt, ye may, Sir.
For you have most command.

MIRABELL

I have seen a wonder.

[Exit.

ORIANA

Is he gone?

FACTOR

Yes.

ORIANA

How?

FACTOR

Taken to the utmost,
A wonder dwells about him.

ORIANA

He did not guess at me?

FACTOR

No, be secure; ye shew another woman,
He is gone to fetch his friends.

ORIANA

Where are the Gentlewomen?

FACTOR

Here, here, now they are come,
Sit still, and let them see ye.

[Enter **ROSALURA**, **LILLIA-BIANCA**, **SERVANT**.

ROSALURA
Pray ye, where's my friend, Sir?

FACTOR
She is within, Ladies, but here's another Gentlewoman,
A stranger to this Town: so please you visit her,
'Twill be well taken.

LILLIA-BIANCA
Where is she?

FACTOR
There, above, Ladies.

SERVANT
'Bless me: what thing is this? two Pinacles
Upon her pate! Is't not a glode to catch Wood-cocks?

ROSALURA
Peace, ye rude knave.

SERVANT
What a bouncing Bum she has too!
There's Sail enough for a Carrack.

ROSALURA
What is this Lady?
For as I live, she's a goodly woman.

FACTOR
Ghess, ghess.

LILLIA-BIANCA
I have not seen a nobler Presence.

SERVANT
'Tis a lustie wench: now could I spend my forty-pence,
With all my heart, to have but one fling at her;
To give her but a washing blow.

LILLIA-BIANCA
Ye Rascal.

SERVANT
I that's all a man has, for's good will: 'twill be long enough,

Before ye cry come Anthonie, and kiss me.

LILLIA-BIANCA
I'le have ye whipt.

ROSALURA
Has my friend seen this Lady?

FACTOR
Yes, yes, and is well known to her.

ROSALURA
I much admire her Presence.

LILLIA-BIANCA
So do I too:
For I protest, she is the handsomest,
The rarest, and the newest to mine eye
That ever I saw yet.

ROSALURA
I long to know her;
My friend shall do that kindness.

ORIANA
So she shall Ladies,
Come, pray ye come up.

ROSALURA
O me.

LILLIA-BIANCA
Hang me if I knew her:
Were I a man my self, I should now love ye;
Nay, I should doat.

ROSALURA
I dare not trust mine eyes;
For as I live ye are the strangest alter'd,
I must come up to know the truth.

SERVANT
So must I, Lady;
For I am a kind of unbeliever too.

LILLIA-BIANCA
Get ye gone, Sirrah;
And what ye have seen, be secret in: you are paid else,

No more of your long tongue.

FACTOR
Will ye go in Ladies,
And talk with her? These venturers will come straight:
Away with this fellow.

LILLIA-BIANCA
There, Sirrah, go, disport ye.

SERVANT
I would the trunk-hos'd-woman would go with me.

[Exit.

SCÆNA QUINTA

Enter **MIRABELL, PINAC, BELLEUR.**

PINAC
Is she so glorious handsom?

MIRABELL
You would wonder:
Our Women look like Gipsies, like Gills to her:
Their Clothes and fashions beggerly, and Bankrupt:
Base, old, and scurvy.

BELLEUR
How looks her face?

MIRABELL
Most heavenly:
And the becoming-motion of her bodie
So sets her off.

BELLEUR
Why then we shall stay.

MIRABELL
Pardon me:
That's more than I know: if she be that woman,
She appears to be.

BELLEUR
As 'tis impossible.

MIRABELL
I shall then tell ye more.

PINAC
Did ye speak to her?

MIRABELL
No, no, I only saw her: She was busie:
Now I go for that end: and mark her, Gentlemen,
If she appear not to ye one of the sweetest,
The handsomest, the fairest in behaviour:
We shall meet the two wenches there too, they come to visit her,
To wonder, as we do.

PINAC
Then we shall meet 'em.

BELLEUR
I had rather meet two Bears.

MIRABELL
There you may take your leaves, dispatch that business,
And as ye find their humours.

PINAC
Is your love there too?

MIRABELL
No certain, she has no great heart to set out again.
This is the house, I'le usher ye.

BELLEUR
I'le bless me,
And take a good heart if I can.

MIRABELL
Come, nobly.

[Exeunt.

SCÆNA SEXTA

Enter **FACTOR, ROSALURA, LILLIA-BIANCA, ORIANA.**

FACTOR

They are come in: Sit you two off, as strangers,
There Ladie: where's the boy? be readie, Sirrah,
And clear your Pipes, the Musick now: they enter.

[Musick.

[Enter **MIRABELL**, **PINAC**, and **BELLEUR**.

PINAC
What a state she keeps! how far off they sit from her!
How rich she is! I marry, this shews bravely.

BELLEUR
She is a lusty wench: and may allure a good man,
But if she have a tongue, I'le not give two pence for her:
There sits my Fury: how I shake to see her!

FACTOR
Madam, this is the Gentleman.

MIRABELL
How sweet she kisses!
She has a Spring dwells on her lips: a paradise:
This is the Legacie.

[SONG.

From the honor'd dead I bring
Thus his love and last offring.
Take it nobly, 'tis your due,
From a friendship ever true.
From a faith &c.

ORIANA
Most noble Sir,
This from my now dead Brother, as his love,
And gratefull memory of your great benefit:
From me my thanks, my wishes, and my service.
Till I am more acquainted I am silent,
Only I dare say this, you are truly noble.

MIRABELL
What should I think?

PINAC
Think ye have a handsom fortune,
Would I had such another.

ROSALURA

Ye are well met Gentlemen,
We hear ye are for travel?

PINAC

Ye hear true, Ladie,
And come to take our leaves.

LILLIA-BIANCA

We'll along with ye,
We see you are grown so witty by your Journey,
We cannot choose but step out too: This Lady
We mean to wait upon as far as Italy.

BELLEUR

I'll travel into Wales, amongst the mountains;
I hope they cannot find me.

ROSALURA

If you go further;
So good, and free society we hold ye,
We'll jog along too.

PINAC

Are ye so valiant Lady?

LILLIA-BIANCA

And we'll be merry, Sir, and laugh.

PINAC

It may be
We'll go by Sea.

LILLIA-BIANCA

Why 'tis the only voyage;
I love a Sea-voyage, and a blustring tempest;
And let all split.

PINAC

This is a dainty Damosel:
I think 'twill tame ye: can ye ride post?

LILLIA-BIANCA

O excellently: I am never weary that way:
A hundred mile a day is nothing with me.

BELLEUR

I'le travel under ground: do you hear (sweet Lady?)

I find it will be dangerous for a woman.

ROSALURA
No danger, Sir, I warrant; I love to be under.

BELLEUR
I see she will abuse me all the world over:
But say we pass through Germany, and drink hard?

ROSALURA
We'll learn to drink and swagger too.

BELLEUR
She'l beat me.
Lady, I'le live at home.

ROSALURA
And I'le live with thee;
And we'll keep house together.

BELLEUR
I'le keep hounds first;
And those I hate right heartily.

PINAC
I go for Turky,
And so it may be up into Persia.

LILLIA-BIANCA
We cannot know too much, I'le travel with ye.

PINAC
And you'l abuse me?

LILLIA-BIANCA
Like enough.

PINAC
'Tis dainty.

BELLEUR
I will live in a bawdy-house.

ROSALURA
I dare come to ye.

BELLEUR
Say, I am dispos'd to hang my self?

ROSALURA
There I'le leave ye.

BELLEUR
I am glad I know how to avoid ye.

MIRABELL
May I speak yet?

FACTOR
She beckons to ye.

MIRABELL
Lady, I could wish, I knew to recompence,
Even with the service of my life, those pains,
And those high favours you have thrown upon me;
Till I be more desertful in your eye;
And till my duty shall make known I honour ye:
Noblest of women, do me but this favour,
To accept this back again, as a poor testimony.

ORIANA
I must have you too with 'em; else the will,
That says they must rest with ye, is infring'd, Sir;
Which pardon me, I dare not do.

MIRABELL
Take me then;
And take me with the truest love.

ORIANA
'Tis certain,
My Brother lov'd ye dearly, and I ought
As dearly to preserve that love. But, Sir,
Though I were willing, these are but your Ceremonies.

MIRABELL
As I have life, I speak my soul.

ORIANA
I like ye.
But how you can like me, without I have Testimony,
A Stranger to ye.

MIRABELL
I'le marry ye immediately,
A fair State I dare promise ye.

BELLEUR
Yet she'll couzen thee.

ORIANA
Would some fair Gentleman durst promise for ye.

MIRABELL
By all that's good.

[Enter **LA-CASTRE**, **NANTOLET**, **LUGIER**, & **De-GARD**.

ALL
And we'll make up the rest, Lady.

ORIANA
Then Oriana takes ye; nay, she has caught ye;
If ye start now let all the world cry shame on ye:
I have out travell'd ye.

BELLEUR
Did not I say she would cheat thee?

MIRABELL
I thank ye, I am pleas'd, ye have deceiv'd me;
And willingly I swallow it, and joy in't;
And yet perhaps I know ye: whose plot was this?

LUGIER
He is not asham'd that cast it: he that executed,
Followed your Fathers will.

MIRABELL
What a world's this, nothing but craft, and cozenage!

ORIANA
Who begun, Sir?

MIRABELL
Well; I do take thee upon meer Compassion;
And I do think, I shall love thee. As a Testimony,
I'le burn my book, and turn a new leaf over,
But these fine clothes you shall wear still.

ORIANA
I obey you, Sir, in all.

NANTOLET

And how! how, daughters! what say you to these Gentlemen?
What say ye, Gentlemen, to the Girles?

PINAC
By my troth—if she can love me.

LILLIA-BIANCA
—How long?

PINAC
Nay, if once ye love.

LILLIA-BIANCA
Then take me,
And take your chance.

PINAC
Most willingly, ye are mine, Lady:
And if I use ye not, that ye may love me.

LILLIA-BIANCA
A Match i' faith.

PINAC
Why now ye travel with me.

ROSALURA
How that thing stands!

BELLEUR
It wlll lf ye urge lt.
'Bless your five wits.

ROSALURA
Nay, 'prethee stay, I'le have thee.

BELLEUR
You must ask me leave first.

ROSALURA
Wilt thou use me kindly;
And beat me but once a week?

BELLEUR
If ye deserve no more.

ROSALURA
And wilt thou get me with child?

BELLEUR
Dost thou ask me seriously?

ROSALURA
Yes indeed do I.

BELLEUR
Yes, I will get thee with child: come presently,
And 't be but in revenge, I'le do thee that courtesie.
Well, if thou wilt fear God, and me; have at thee.

ROSALURA
I'le love ye, and I'le honour ye.

BELLEUR
I am pleas'd then.

MIRABELL
This Wild-Goose Chase is done, we have won o' both sides.
Brother, your love: and now to Church of all hands;
Let's lose no time.

PINAC
Our travelling, lay by.

BELLEUR
No more for Italy; for the Low-Countries.

[Exeunt.

John Fletcher – A Short Biography

John Fletcher was born in December, 1579 in Rye, Sussex. He was baptised on December 20th.

As can be imagined details of much of his life and career have not survived and, accordingly, only a very brief indication of his life and works can be given.

His father, Richard Fletcher, was a successful and rather ambitious cleric. From being the Dean of Peterborough he moved on to become the Bishop of Bristol, Bishop of Worcester and finally, shortly before his death, the Bishop of London. He was also the chaplain to Queen Elizabeth.

When he was Dean of Peterborough, Richard Fletcher, witnessed the execution of Mary, Queen of Scots. It was said he "knelt down on the scaffold steps and started to pray out loud and at length, in a prolonged and rhetorical style, as though determined to force his way into the pages of history". He cried out at her death, "So perish all the Queen's enemies!" All very dramatic but the family did have strong links to the Arts.

Young Fletcher appears at the very young age of eleven to have entered Corpus Christi College at Cambridge University in 1591. There are no records that he ever took a degree but there is some small evidence that he was being prepared for a career in the church.

However what is clear is that this was soon abandoned as he joined the stream of people who would leave University and decamp to the more bohemian life of commercial theatre in London.

Unfortunately his father fell out with Queen Elizabeth but appears to have been on his way to rehabilitation before his death in 1596. At his death he was, however, mired in debt.

The upbringing of the now teenage Fletcher and his seven siblings now passed to his paternal uncle, the poet and minor official Giles Fletcher. Giles, who had the patronage of the Earl of Essex may have been a liability rather than an advantage to the young Fletcher. With Essex involved in the failed rebellion against Elizabeth Giles was also tainted by association.

By 1606 John Fletcher appears to have equipped himself with the talents to become a playwright. Initially this appears to have been for the Children of the Queen's Revels, then performing at the Blackfriars Theatre.

Commendatory verses by Richard Brome in the Beaumont and Fletcher 1647 folio place Fletcher in the company of Ben Jonson, although it is not known when this friendship began. Jonson, of course, was a leviathan of English Literature, so admired that many of his literary friends and colleagues were simply known as 'Sons of Ben'. Fletcher's frequent early collaborator, Francis Beaumont, was also a friend of Jonson's.

Fletcher's early career was marked by one significant failure; The Faithful Shepherdess, his adaptation of Giovanni Battista Guarini's Il Pastor Fido, which was performed by the Blackfriars Children in 1608. In the preface to the printed edition of his play, Fletcher explained the failure as due to his audience's faulty expectations. They expected a pastoral tragicomedy to feature dances, comedy, and murder, with the shepherds presented in conventional stereotypes – as Fletcher put it, wearing "gray cloaks, with curtailed dogs in strings." Fletcher's preface is however best known for its pithy definition of tragicomedy: "A tragicomedy is not so called in respect of mirth and killing, but in respect it wants [i.e., lacks] deaths, which is enough to make it no tragedy; yet brings some near it, which is enough to make it no comedy." A comedy, he went on to say, must be "a representation of familiar people." His preface is critical of drama that features characters whose action violates nature.

In that case, Fletcher appears to have been developing a new style faster than audiences could comprehend. By 1609, however, he had found his stride. With Beaumont, he wrote Philaster, which became a hit for the King's Men and began a profitable association between Fletcher and that company. Philaster appears also to have begun a trend for tragicomedy. Fletcher's influence has also been said to have inspired some features of Shakespeare's late romances, and certainly his influence on the tragicomic work of other playwrights is even more marked.

By the middle of the 1610s, Fletcher's plays had achieved a popularity that rivalled Shakespeare's and cemented the pre-eminence of the King's Men in Jacobean London. After Beaumont's retirement, necessitated by ill-health, and then his early death in 1616, Fletcher continued working, both singly and in collaboration, until his death in 1625. By that time, he had produced, or had been credited with, close to fifty plays. This body of work remained a major part of the King's Men's repertory until the closing of the theatres in 1642 due to the Civil War.

At the beginning of his career Fletcher's most important collaborator was Francis Beaumont. The two wrote together for close to a decade, first for the Children of the Queen's Revels, and then for the King's Men. According to an anecdote transmitted or invented by John Aubrey, they also lived together in Bankside, sharing clothes and having "one wench in the house between them." This domestic arrangement, if it existed, was ended by Beaumont's marriage in 1613, and their dramatic partnership ended after Beaumont fell ill, probably of a stroke, that same year.

At this point Fletcher had written many plays with Beaumont and several others on his own. He seems to have been regarded as quite a talent although it should be remembered that playwrights were required to be prolific, to easily work with other collaborators and to produce work of quality and commercial appeal very quickly.

The King's Men, run by Philip Henslowe, was the most prestigious of the theatre companies and Fletcher now had an increasingly close association with it.

Fletcher collaborated with Shakespeare on Henry VIII, The Two Noble Kinsmen, and the now lost Cardenio, which some scholars say was the basis for Lewis Theobald's play Double Falsehood. (Theobald is regarded as one of the best Shakespearean editors. Whether his play is based on Cardenio or on some other is not absolutely known although Theobald certainly promoted it as his revision of the lost Shakespeare/Fletcher play.)

A play that Fletcher also wrote by himself at this time, The Woman's Prize or the Tamer Tamed, is also regarded as a sequel to The Taming of the Shrew.

In 1616, with the death of Shakespeare, Fletcher now appears to have entered into an enhanced arrangement with the King's Men on very similar terms to Shakespeare's. Fletcher would now write exclusively for the King's Men until his own death almost a decade later.

As well as continuing his solo productions Fletcher was still collaborating with other playwrights, mainly Philip Massinger, who, in turn, would succeed him as the in-house playwright for the King's Men.

Fletcher's popularity continued throughout his life; indeed during the winter of 1621, he had three of his plays performed at court. His mastery is most notable in two dramatic types; tragicomedy and the comedy of manners.

John Fletcher died in 1625, it is thought of bubonic plague which, at the time, was undergoing further outbreaks.

He seems to have been buried in what is now Southwark Cathedral, although a precise location is not known. There is much made of an anecdote that Fletcher and Massinger (who died in 1640) share the same grave but it is more likely that both are buried within a few yards of each other and that the stone markers in the floor have confused the issue. One is marked 'Edmond Shakespeare 1607' and the other 'John Fletcher 1625' refers to Shakespeare's younger brother and the playwright. The churchyards were, more often than not, completely over-crowded and breeding grounds for disease. Precise record keeping was not a practiced skill.

During the later Commonwealth, many of the playwright's best-known scenes were kept alive as drolls. These were brief performances, usually condensed into one or two scenes and with the addition of music or song to satisfy the taste for plays while the theatres were closed under the Puritans. At the re-opening of the theatres in 1660, the plays in the Fletcher canon, in original form or revised, were by far the most common productions on the English stage. The most frequently revived plays suggest the developing taste for comedies of manners. Among the tragedies, The Maid's Tragedy and, especially, Rollo Duke of Normandy held the stage. Four tragicomedies (A King and No King, The Humorous Lieutenant, Philaster, and The Island Princess) were popular, perhaps in part for their similarity to and foreshadowing of heroic drama. Four comedies (Rule a Wife And Have a Wife, The Chances, Beggars' Bush, and especially The Scornful Lady) were also stage mainstays.

Despite his popularity, and it appears he was held in higher regard than Shakespeare at this time, his works steadily lost ground to those of Shakespeare and to new productions from other playwrights.

Since then Fletcher has increasingly become a subject only for occasional revivals and for specialists. Fletcher and his collaborators have been the subject of important bibliographic and critical studies, but the plays have been revived only infrequently.

Due to the frequent collaborations between all manner of playwrights, and the revisions carried out in later years, having a settled list of authorship to any given set of plays can be problematic. The works of Fletcher and others of this period most definitely fall into this category. It is as well to take into account that during this period theatres were quite often closed either due to outbreaks of the plague or to the prevailing political and moral climate. Printers, anxious to provide materials that would sell, were not above changing a name or two to enhance sales.

Although Fletcher collaborated most often with Beaumont and Massinger, it is believed that Massinger revised many of the plays some time after their original production. Other collaborators including Nathan Field, William Shakespeare, William Rowley and others also can be seen distinctly in Fletchers' works. Many modern scholars point out that Fletcher had many particular mannerisms but other playwrights would also duplicate these at times so allocating exact contributions of anyone to a play is somewhat of a detective case in many instances. However from the original folio printings or licensing via the Master of the Revels (the statutory licensing authority to approve and censor plays as well a hand in publication and printing of theatrical materials) as well as contemporary notes a fairly precise bibliography of the works can be given with only a few plays lacking substantial authority and provenance.

John Fletcher – A Concise Bibliography

This bibliography gives the most likely date of writing together with when published, revised or licensed by the Master or the Revels (This position within the royal household was originally for royal festivities, ie revels, and later to oversee stage censorship, until this function was transferred to the Lord Chamberlain in 1624).

Solo Plays

The Faithful Shepherdess, pastoral (written 1608–9; printed 1609)
The Tragedy of Valentinian, tragedy (1610–14; 1647)
Monsieur Thomas, comedy (c. 1610–16; 1639)
The Woman's Prize, or The Tamer Tamed, comedy (c. 1611; 1647)
Bonduca, tragedy (1611–14; 1647)
The Chances, comedy (c. 1613–25; 1647)
Wit Without Money, comedy (c. 1614; 1639)
The Mad Lover, tragicomedy (acted 5 January 1617; 1647)
The Loyal Subject, tragicomedy (licensed 16 November 1618; revised 1633; 1647)
The Humorous Lieutenant, tragicomedy (c. 1619; 1647)
Women Pleased, tragicomedy (c. 1619–23; 1647)
The Island Princess, tragicomedy (c. 1620; 1647)
The Wild Goose Chase, comedy (c. 1621; 1652)
The Pilgrim, comedy (c. 1621; 1647)
A Wife for a Month, tragicomedy (licensed 27 May 1624; 1647)
Rule a Wife and Have a Wife, comedy (licensed 19 October 1624; 1640)

Collaborations

With Francis Beaumont

The Woman Hater, comedy (1606; 1607)
Cupid's Revenge, tragedy (c. 1607–12; 1615)
Philaster, or Love Lies a-Bleeding, tragicomedy (c. 1609; 1620)
The Maid's Tragedy, Tragedy (c. 1609; 1619)
A King and No King, tragicomedy (1611; 1619)
The Captain, comedy (c. 1609–12; 1647)
The Scornful Lady, comedy (c. 1613; 1616)
Love's Pilgrimage, tragicomedy (c. 1615–16; 1647)
The Noble Gentleman, comedy (c. 1613; licensed 3 February 1626; 1647)

With Francis Beaumont & Philip Massinger

Thierry & Theodoret, tragedy (c. 1607; 1621)
The Coxcomb, comedy (c. 1608–10; 1647)
Beggars' Bush, comedy (c. 1612–13; revised 1622; 1647)
Love's Cure, comedy (c. 1612–13; revised 1625; 1647)

With Philip Massinger

Sir John van Olden Barnavelt, tragedy (August 1619; MS)
The Little French Lawyer, comedy (c. 1619–23; 1647)
A Very Woman, tragicomedy (c. 1619–22; licensed 6 June 1634; 1655)
The Custom of the Country, comedy (c. 1619–23; 1647)
The Double Marriage, tragedy (c. 1619–23; 1647)
The False One, history (c. 1619–23; 1647)
The Prophetess, tragicomedy (licensed 14 May 1622; 1647)
The Sea Voyage, comedy (licensed 22 June 1622; 1647)
The Spanish Curate, comedy (licensed 24 October 1622; 1647)

The Lovers' Progress or The Wandering Lovers, tragicomedy (licensed 6 December 1623; rev 1634; 1647)
The Elder Brother, comedy (c. 1625; 1637)

With Philip Massinger & Nathan Field
The Honest Man's Fortune, tragicomedy (1613; 1647)
The Queen of Corinth, tragicomedy (c. 1616–18; 1647)
The Knight of Malta, tragicomedy (c. 1619; 1647)

With William Shakespeare
Henry VIII, history (c. 1613; 1623)
The Two Noble Kinsmen, tragicomedy (c. 1613; 1634)
Cardenio, tragicomedy (c. 1613)

With Thomas Middleton & William Rowley
Wit at Several Weapons, comedy (c. 1610–20; 1647)

With William Rowley
The Maid in the Mill (licensed 29 August 1623; 1647).

With Nathan Field
Four Plays, or Moral Representations, in One, morality (c. 1608–13; 1647)

With Philip Massinger, Ben Jonson and George Chapman
Rollo Duke of Normandy, or The Bloody Brother, tragedy (c. 1617; revised 1627–30; 1639)

With James Shirley
The Night Walker, or The Little Thief, comedy (c. 1611; 1640)
The Coronation c. 1635

Uncertain
The Nice Valour, or The Passionate Madman, comedy (c. 1615–25; 1647)
The Laws of Candy, tragicomedy (c. 1619–23; 1647)
The Fair Maid of the Inn, comedy (licensed 22 January 1626; 1647)
The Faithful Friends, tragicomedy (registered 29 June 1660; MS.)

The Nice Valour is possibly by Fletcher revised by Thomas Middleton;

The Fair Maid of the Inn is perhaps a play by Massinger, John Ford, and John Webster, either with or without Fletcher's involvement.

The Laws of Candy has been variously attributed to Fletcher and to John Ford.

The Night-Walker was a Fletcher original, with additions by Shirley for a 1639 production.

Even now there is not absolute certainty on several of the plays. The first Beaumont & Fletcher folio of 1647 contained 35 plays and the second folio of 1679 added a further 18. In total 53 plays.

The first folio included The Masque of the Inner Temple and Gray's Inn (1613), and the second The Knight of the Burning Pestle (1607), widely considered Beaumont's solo works, although the latter was in early editions attributed to both writers. Fletcher himself said that Beaumont was attributed so-authorship of many works that belonged solely to Fletcher or to other collaborators.

One play in the canon, Sir John Van Olden Barnavelt, existed in manuscript and was not published till 1883.